Greco-Roman Literature and the New Testament

SOCIETY OF BIBLICAL LITERATURE
Sources for Biblical Study

Edited by
Bernard Brandon Scott

Number 21
Greco-Roman Literature and the New Testament

Edited by
David E. Aune

GRECO-ROMAN LITERATURE AND THE NEW TESTAMENT:
Selected Forms and Genres

Edited by
David E. Aune

Scholars Press
Atlanta, Georgia

Greco-Roman Literature and the New Testament

© 1988
The Society of Biblical Literature

LIBRARY OF CONGRESS
Library of Congress Cataloging-in-Publication Data

Aune, David Edward.
  Greco-Roman literature and the New Testament : selected forms and genres / David E. Aune.
  p. cm. — (Sources for biblical study; no. 21)

  1. Bible. N.T.—Criticism, Form. 2. Greek literature, Hellenistic—History and criticism. 3. Literary form. I. Title. II. Series.
BS2377.A9 1987
225.6'6—dc19   87-34007
ISBN: 1-55540-231-3   CIP
ISBN: 1-55540-209-7 (pbk)
              Printed in the United States of America
                       on acid-free paper

TABLE OF CONTENTS

Introduction... vi

Chapter 1: The Chreia 1
    Vernon K. Robbins
    Emory University

Chapter 2: Household Codes............................ 25
    David L. Balch
    Brite Divinity School
    Texas Christian University

Chapter 3: The Ancient Jewish Synagogue Homily........... 51
    William Richard Stegner
    Garrett-Evangelical Theological Seminary

Chapter 4: The Diatribe 71
    Stanley K. Stowers
    Brown University

Chapter 5: Ancient Greek Letters........................ 85
    John L. White
    Loyola University of Chicago

Chapter 6: Greco-Roman Biography...................... 107
    David E. Aune
    Saint Xavier College

Chapter 7: The Greek Novel 127
    Ronald F. Hock
    University of Southern California

INTRODUCTION

Early Christianity emerged from Judaism, and it is therefore natural that the literature of ancient Israel and of early Judaism has traditionally been recognized as valuable sources for promoting a more adequate understanding of the New Testament and early Christian literature. Yet it must also be kept in mind that the New Testament was written in *Greek*, the language of government, trade and culture throughout most of the Roman empire. By the sixth decade of the first century A.D., Christianity had already spread to every major urban area of the Roman world, a world unified politically and economically under the Roman empire, but a world which was dominated by Hellenistic culture. In recent years the potential relevance of Greco-Roman literature for the student of the New Testament has become increasingly evident. The purpose of this collection of essays is to demonstrate both the relevance and importance of various styles, forms and genres of ancient Mediterranean literature for the understanding and interpretation of the New Testament. Most of the forms and genres discussed in the following chapters are drawn from pagan Hellenistic literary culture. The exception is the analysis of "The Ancient Jewish Synagogue Homily" by Professor W. R. Stegner. The importance of this genre for students of the New Testament, coupled with the anachronistic way in which this genre has often been used to interpret sections of the New Testament, has led to its inclusion in this collection of essays.

Each of the following chapters has been written by a New Testament scholar who has also specialized in the study of a particular type of ancient literature which lends itself to comparison with the New Testament and early Christian literature. All of the contributors are teachers who have used the kinds of materials presented here in the classroom to enlarge the horizons of students of the New Testament to the riches which lie buried in neglected texts from the Hellenistic world. The central purpose of each essay is to demonstrate the relevance and fruitfulness of reading and comparing the New Testament with a variety of such texts. Each essay is written with the student in mind, and is intended to function as a supplementary text in introductory courses in New Testament literature. The essays are designed to provoke reflection and discussion and to provide guidance for further study.

The following seven chapters are in no sense exhaustive, but represent simply a selection of ancient forms and genres which appear most relevant for students of the New Testament. There is always the danger that those whose primary interest is early Christian literature will seize only the more easily portable valuables found in random raids on ancient texts. The contributors to this volume disagree with that superficial approach. All ancient texts are part of a cultural system, and must be understood in context and with integrity if they are to be properly evaluated. That is why the context for comparison emphasized in the following pages is not simply the individual word or phrase or the isolated theme or motif, but rather textual units of varying size and complexity which can be described as literary forms or genres.

Each of the following chapters focuses on the respective contributor's English translation of a text or texts which has either not been translated before or else is not readily available. These translations are accompanied by notes or explanations intended to make some of the more important or obscure features of the text readily comprehensible. The translated texts themselves are introduced by a survey of the recent history of research as well as by a discussion of the major generic features of the particular form or genre represented. After dealing with these four tasks, the contributors then tackle with the problem of relating these texts to the understanding and interpretation of various aspects of the New Testament. The concluding section of each chapter contains an annotated bibliography designed to guide the reader into a deeper and more detailed consideration of each literary form or genre treated. Not all of the essays rigidly conform to the structure just outlined. In Professor V. K. Robbins' treatment of "The Chreia," the brief and varied nature of the literary form in question has required a different though basically compatible approach.

D. E. Aune

CHAPTER 1
THE CHREIA

Vernon K. Robbins
Emory University

I. Introduction

Almost every person knows and occasionally recites a maxims like "Better late than never," "Nothing ventured nothing gained," or "A penny saved is a penny earned." Fewer people attribute a saying or action to a specific person as they recite it. When there are summaries of particular people's activities on radio or TV, in newspapers or magazines, in speeches on special occasions, or in sermons, we may encounter the recital of a saying or action attributed to a specific person. For example, we might read or hear: John F. Kennedy, on the day of his inauguration, said: "Ask not what your country can do for you; ask what you can do for your country"; or: Martin Luther King, on the day before his death, said: "I've been to the mountaintop; I've looked over; and I've seen the promised land."[1] Another could be: Adolf Hitler, when the black athlete Jesse Owens won four gold medals in a single day at the Olympic games, walked out of the stadium.[2] Or still another could be: George Washington, when his father asked him, "Do you know who cut down my cherry tree?", replied, "I did it, father. I cannot tell a lie. I cut down your cherry tree."[3]

During the time when Christians were writing, re-writing, and copying the documents we find in the NT and early Christian literature, rhetoricians and teachers used the term chreia to refer to a saying or act attributed to a specific person (the Greek word chreia rhymes with "play

---

[1] These are based on the speeches as printed in: Theodore Sorensen, *Kennedy* (New York: Harper & Row, 1965) 248; and *A Testament of Hope: The Essential Writings on Martin Luther King, Jr.* (ed. James M. Washington; San Francisco: Harper & Row, 1986) 286.

[2] This is based on: Jesse Owens, *I Have Changed* (New York: Wm. Morrow & Company, 1972) 18-19.

[3] This is based on: Augusta Stevenson, *George Washington, Boy Leader* (Indianapolis/New York: Bobbs-Merrill Company, 1959).

a," and the plural chreiai rhymes with "may I").[4] Aelius Theon of Alexandria, a rhetorician who produced a textbook for teachers during the time in which the NT gospels were being written (ca. 50–100 CE), wrote the following example of a chreia: "Diogenes the philosopher, on being asked by someone how he could become famous, responded: 'By worrying as little as possible about fame'" (Hock-O'Neil 85 [Chreia 22]). We get our most specific information about the chreia from textbooks called *Progymnasmata* (Preliminary Exercises) that were written by various rhetoricians during the first through the fifth centuries CE.

II. Defining the Chreia

According to the textbooks written by rhetoricians, a chreia can be defined as "a saying or act that is well-aimed or apt, expressed concisely, attributed to a person, and regarded as useful for living."[5] This means that a chreia is a particular type of reminiscence. We might think of a reminiscence as an anecdote which is "a narrative, usually brief, of an interesting, often amusing, incident or event."[6] People in late antiquity, however, distinguished a chreia from a narrative about an event.[7] They considered the content of a chreia to be a well-aimed or apt statement or

---

[4]The singular in Latin is *chria* (rhymes with "be a"), and the plural is *chriae* (rhymes with "bee eye").

[5]Cf. Ronald F. Hock and Edward N. O'Neil (eds.), *The Chreia in Ancient Rhetoric*, Vol. 1: *The Progymnasmata* (Texts and Translations 27; Atlanta: Scholars Press, 1986), 26. Interpreters have had considerable discussion over the meaning of the phrases which here are translated "well-aimed or apt." The earliest source, Aelius Theon (ca. 50–100 CE), has *met' eustochias* ("with a well-aimed or apt quality") between "a concise statement or action" and "attributed to some specified character." This position for the prepositional phrase raises debate whether it modifies the preceding and means "statement or action with a well-aimed quality" or modifies the succeeding and means "with aptness attributed to some specified character." In my view, the following authors were emphasizing the "well-aimed" quality of the statement or action in a context in which they presupposed the aptness of the attribution: Hermogenes *(echon dēlōsin)*; Nicolaus *(eustochos kai suntomos)*; Priscian *(celerum habens demonstrationem)*. Aphthonius, on the other hand, emphasizes the "aptness" of the attribution *(eustochōs epi ti prosōpon anapherousa)*. The discussions in the Hock-O'Neil volume emphasize the aptness of the attribution, which is an essential quality of the chreia. The aptness must be emphasized in our culture, which regularly emphasizes ideas without interest in people who inaugurated or focussed those ideas. The aptness, however, must not be emphasized at the expense of the well-aimed quality. If a concise statement or action simply is aptly attributed, it may be an "informative" reminiscence without being a chreia. An apt and well-aimed reminiscence, on the other hand, is a chreia, like: Plato said that the Muses dwell in the souls of the gifted (Chreia 52 in Hock-O'Neil) or Diogenes, on seeing a youth misbehaving, beat the paedagogus (Chreia 26 in Hock-O'Neil). These are chreiai, because they have aptness and pointedness which discloses the persons to whom they are attributed and focuses one's thought on particular aspects of life.

[6]*Webster's New Collegiate Dictionary* (2d ed.; Springfield, Mass.: G. & C. Merrian Co., 1956) 34.

[7]The rhetoricians in late antiquity would consider these to be either narratives or fables.

action attributed to a particular person. The emphasis on the particular person gave the chreia a special place in the transmission of Hellenic-Roman heritage. According to one estimate, we have available in writing perhaps a thousand chreiai from antiquity.[8] Many people knew and recited chreiai,[9] and, as a result, they transmitted a rich heritage of Hellenic-Roman culture. If this chapter included a large number of chreiai like the four constructed for the opening paragraph, it would transmit significant segments of American culture.[10]

The special interest in the chreia appears to lie in its special qualities, and we may begin to appreciate these qualities if we see how elusive the nature of the chreia has been for interpreters during the twentieth century. In 1901, G. von Wartensleben concentrated on the chreia in Greek philosophical writing[11] but also devoted sections to Machon's chreiai (3d cent. BCE)[12] and the rhetorical schools.[13] Wartensleben listed three characteristics for the chreia:

(1) Unconditioned brevity and vigorousness of the statement or act.

(2) Attribution of the act or statement to a definite person.

(3) Judgement that the act or statement is something useful.

Items (2) and (3) are well-stated. But there are two challenges in item (1). Firstly, when interpreters emphasize the "unconditioned brevity" of the chreia, they regularly overlook chreiai which exist in expanded form, chreiai which have comments or objections appended, and chreiai which are part of an argumentative refutation or confirmation. We will see below that, although people regularly cite chreiai in an abbreviated form, chreiai are formulated in various lengths and forms to function well in a variety of settings in discourse. Secondly, interpreters have not investigated the range of dynamics in the "vigorousness of the statement or the act." Part of the difficulty, it appears, has been the lack of awareness that the vigorousness must be explored from two angles. On the one hand, the vigorousness emerges from the "aim" of the statement or act. The saying or act points at something, but that to which it points may be highly elusive. It may aim simply at humor or wordplay, or it may aim at some attribute of behavior or some philosophical or religious principle. This range of targets makes the chreia a slippery, intriguing, and compel-

---

[8] Henry A. Fischel, "Studies in Cynicism and the Ancient Near East: The Transformation of a Chria." In J. Neusner (ed.), *Religions in Antiquity: Essays in Memory of E. R. Goodenough.* (Leiden: Brill, 1968), 374; cited in Hock-O'Neil 3.

[9] Hock-O'Neil 7.

[10] It is not accidental that my wife, Deanna Robbins, who is a kindergarten teacher, was able in about an hour to get books which would enable me to write the chreiai in the opening paragraph in accord with authoritative tradition in American society.

[11] G. von Wartensleben, *Begriff der griechischen Chreia und Beiträge ihrer Form* (Heidelberg: Winter, 1901), 27–125.

[12] Ibid., 125–38.

[13] Ibid., 138–42.

ling form. The chreia is so interesting, because it continually escapes attempts to capture it through analysis. On the other hand, the vigorousness of the statement or act emerges from its "apt" attribution to the person who is the subject of the chreia. It would be hard to overemphasize the attribution of the chreia to a particular person, because this is *the* aspect which distinguishes it from other forms. An unattributed saying or an interesting event may be "well-aimed"; in other words, its import may be humorous, virtuous, religious, or philosophical. But the attribution of a saying or act to a particular person displays aspects of life, thought, and action in a mode which integrates attitudes, values, and concepts with personal, social, and cultural realities. The people featured in chreiai become authoritative media of positive and negative truths about life. These "authorities" transmit social, cultural, religious, and philosophical heritage into later historical epochs.

III. Classifying Chreiai

While the rhetoricians definition of the chreia differentiates it from proverbs and reminiscences of interesting or amusing incidents, their system of classification helps us to understand the basic parts of the chreia. Rhetoricians classified chreiai according to the presence or absence of speech and action in the beginning part and the final part. First of all, rhetoricians distinguished between "sayings" chreiai and "action" chreiai. Three of our examples in the opening paragraph are sayings chreiai, while the one about Hitler is an action chreia. The rhetorician Theon, referred to above, identified two species of sayings chreiai, the statement and the response species, and his discussion helps us to understand the potential presence or absence of speech or action in the two parts of the chreia. Instances of the statement species may differ from one another by the presence or absence of a specified situation for the saying of the person. In Theon's words, a chreia may have "an unprompted statement," that is, it may attribute the saying to a particular person without describing a specific situation. Theon gives the following example:

> Isocrates the sophist used to say that gifted students are children of the gods. (Hock-O'Neil 84 [Chreia 40])

In this chreia, the saying occurs in a situation characterized only by the lifetime of Isocrates the sophist. A later manuscript contains a chreia which gives a general description of the situation:

> Pythagoras the philosopher, once he had disembarked and was teaching writings, used to counsel his students to abstain from red meat. (Hock-O'Neil 335 [Chreia 55])

The Chreia

In this instance, the saying is attributed to Pythagoras during a certain period of his lifetime, namely after he had left and was teaching writing. Still, there is no *specific* situation. A similar reference to a period of time occurs in this chreia in the New Testament:

> Now after John was arrested, Jesus came into Galilee, preaching the gospel of God, and saying, "The time is fulfilled, and the kingdom of God is at hand; repent, and believe in the gospel. (Mark 1:14–15)

Theon would, it appears, have classified this as an unprompted statement, since the description of the situation does not include a specific time to which Jesus responded when he saw it.

In contrast, Theon writes, some statements arise out of specific circumstances. Characteristically, the statement emerges as the result of "seeing" something. Theon gives the following example:

> Diogenes the Cynic philosopher, on seeing a rich man who was uneducated said: "This fellow is silver-plated filth." (Hock-O'Neil 85 [Chreia 23])

This kind of statement species also is found in the New Testament:

> And passing along by the Sea of Galilee, he [Jesus] saw Simon and Andrew the brother of Simon casting a net in the sea; for they were fishermen. And Jesus said to them, "Follow me and I will make you become fishers of men." (Mk 1:16–17)

In this instance, Jesus saw people engaged in a specific activity, and his statement arises out of this situation.

A sayings chreia may belong to the "response" species rather than the "statement" species, according to Theon. This means that some kind of speech occurs or is referred to in the situation prior to the saying. Theon distinguishes four kinds of response species, and these distinctions help us to see a range of possibilities in the speech in a chreia. The first kind of response species contains a question in the situation which may be answered simply by yes or no. Theon's example is:

> Pittacus of Mitylene, on being asked if anyone escapes the notice of the gods in committing some sinful act, said: "No, not even in contemplating it." (Hock-O'Neil 85 [Chreia 49])

Theon says that Pittacus simply could have said "no" without adding the comment about contemplating the act. Our search thus far in the NT has not produced an example of this kind of response species. The next kind, however, is widespread. It contains an inquiry in the situation which requires the speaker to provide some kind of information beyond yes or no. Theon's example is:

> Theano the Pythagorean philosopher, on being asked by someone how long after intercourse with a man does a woman go in purity to the Thesmophorion, said, "With your own, immediately; with another's, never." (Hock-O'Neil 87 [Chreia 64])

Some examples from the New Testament are as follows:

> And the multitudes asked him [John the Baptist], "What then shall we do?" And he answered them, "He who has two coats, let him share with him who has none; and he who has food, let him do likewise." (Lk 3:10–11)

> Tax collectors also came to be baptized, and said to him [John the Baptist], "Teacher, what shall we do?" And he said to them, "Collect no more than is appointed you." (Lk 3:12–13)

> Soldiers also asked him [John the Baptist], "And we, what shall we do?" And he said to them, "Rob no one by violence or by false accusation, and be content with your wages." (Lk 3:14)

Another kind of "response" species includes an explanation, advice, or some such thing in addition to the answer to the question. Theon gives the following example:

> Socrates, on being asked whether the Persian king seemed happy to him, said, "I can't say, for I can't know where he stands on education." (Hock-O'Neil 87 [Chreia 57])

An example in the NT is as follows:

> He [Jesus] went on his way through towns and villages, teaching, and journeying toward Jerusalem. And some one said to him, "Lord, will those who are saved be few?" And he said to them, "Strive to enter by the narrow door; for many, I tell you, will seek to enter and will not be able." (Lk 13:22–24)

In both of these examples, the saying includes an explanation for the very first words he said in response. Still another kind of "response" chreia contains simply a remark in the situation rather than a simple question or inquiry to which the response is made. Theon gives the following example:

> Once when Diogenes was having lunch in the marketplace and invited him to lunch, Plato said, "Diogenes, how charming your unpretentiousness would be, if it were not so pretentious." (Hock-O'Neil 87 [Chreia 50])

In this instance, the chreia says that Diogenes "invited" Plato rather than "asked" him something. It is important to see that even if Diogenes would have invited him by saying, "Will you have lunch with me?", this would not be an instance of a simple question or inquiry, since the question does not seek information about some topic. Thus, Theon is looking into the substance of the interaction rather than simply at formal characteristics. An example of a response to a remark in the NT is:

> Now when Jesus saw great crowds around him, he gave orders to go over to the other side. And a scribe came up and said to him, "Teacher, I will follow you wherever you go." And Jesus said to him, "Foxes have holes, and birds of the air have nests; but the Son of man has nowhere to lay his head." (Mt 8:18–20)

Sayings chreiai, then, may or may not contain specific information about a situation in which the saying occurs, though they always place the saying in the setting of a particular person's life. These chreiai may contain a topical question which can be answered by yes or no, by information, or by a saying including an explanation or some additional comment; or a remark may be the occasion for the response.

Theon calls the final kind of sayings chreia a "double" chreia. This kind contains two sayings, each of which could make a separate chreia. His example is:

> Alexander the Macedonian king stood over Diogenes as he slept and said (Iliad 2.24),
> "To sleep all night ill-suits a counsellor." And Diogenes responded (Iliad 2.25),
> "On whom the folk rely, whose cares are many." (Hock-O'Neil 87 [Chreia 24])

An example in the NT is:

> Then Jesus came from Galilee to the Jordan to John, to be baptized by him. John would have prevented him, saying "I need to be baptized by you, and do you come to me?" But Jesus answered him, "Let it be so now; for thus it is fitting for us to fulfill all righteousness." (Mt 3:13–15)

The "double" nature of this chreia is well-preserved in the version found in the Gospel of the Ebionites 4:

> And then it saith,
> (1) John fell down before him [Jesus] and said: "I beseech thee, Lord, baptize thou me."
> (2) But he [Jesus] prevented him and said: "Suffer it; for thus it is fitting that everything should be fulfilled." (Epiphanius Haer. 30.13.7–8)

In these instances, two individual people make a statement, and each statement could exist as a separate chreia.[14]

The first basic class of chreia, then, is the "sayings" chreia. These may or may not contain a specific situation, though they always contain attribution to a particular person. Also, they may contain a topical question or simply a remark in the first part to which the saying responds. In addition, it is possible to have a "double" chreia where two people make statements and either statement could make a separate chreia.

The second basic class of chreia is the "action" chreia. Theon's discussion of this class calls attention to the chreia's potential for action either in the situation or the response. An action chreia may be either active or passive. Theon's example of an active action chreia is:

> Diogenes the Cynic philosopher, on seeing a boy who was a gourmand, struck the paedagogus with his staff. (Hock-O'Neil 89 [Chreia 25])

His example of a passive action chreia is:

> Didymon the flute-player, on being convicted of adultery, was hanged by his namesake. (Hock-O'Neil 89 [Chreia 21])

There are not many chreiai which simply are action chreiai. Rather, they contain both speech and action. Thus, Theon immediately discusses the third class of chreia, the "mixed" chreia which contains both speech and action. Theon gives two examples:

> Pythagoras the philosopher, on being asked how long human life is, went up to his bedroom and peeked in for a short time, showing thereby its brevity. (Hock-O'Neil 89 [Chreia 54])

> A Laconian, when someone asked him where the Lacedaemonians consider the boundaries of their land to be, showed his spear. (Hock-O'Neil 89 [Chreia 45])

Theon's examples feature speech in the situation and action in the response. But later rhetoricians considered a mixed chreia to contain both speech and action in the response. Hermogenes' example (2d cent. CE) is:

> Diogenes, on seeing a youth misbehaving, beat the paedagogus and said, "Why were you teaching such things?" (Hock-O'Neil 175 [Chreia 261])

---

[14] Ign. Smyr. 1:1 has it in the form: [He was] baptized by John that "all righteousness might be fulfilled."

In this instance, Diogenes responded with an action of beating and with a statement. Many chreiai in the New Testament are mixed chreiai, sometimes containing action and speech in both the situation and the response. Some examples are as follows:

> At that time the disciples came to Jesus, saying, "Who is the greatest in the kingdom of heaven?" And calling to him a child, he put him in the midst of them, and said, "Truly, I say to you, unless you turn and become like children, you will never enter the kingdom of heaven." (Mt 18:1-3)
>
> And he entered the temple and began to drive out those who sold, saying to them, "It is written, 'My house shall be a house of prayer'; but you have made it a den of robbers." (Lk 19:45-46)
>
> While he was still speaking to the people, behold, his mother and his brothers stood outside, asking to speak to him. But he replied to the man who told him, "Who is my mother, and who are my brothers?" And stretching out his hand toward his disciples, he said, "Here are my mother and my brothers! For whoever does the will of my Father in heaven is my brother, and sister, and mother." (Mt 12:46-50)

The identification of active and passive actions, and of combinations of speech and actions, gives us deeper insight into the nature of chreiai. On the one hand, units in which things happen to Jesus may be passive action chreiai. An example is:

> The Spirit immediately drove him [Jesus] out into the wilderness, and he was in the wilderness forty days tempted by Satan, and he was with wild beasts, and the angels ministered to him. (Mk 1:12-13)

When an interpreter knows the potential for a chreia to be passive in nature, he or she can see how the action upon Jesus by the Spirit coordinates with the action upon Jesus by Satan and climaxes in the action upon Jesus by the angels. The unit is a passive action chreia which shows that Jesus possesses powerful resources for good against evil. In contrast, the passive chreia about Didymon above shows the evil nature of an adulterous flute player. Rhetoric which praises good and censures evil was called "epideictic" rhetoric by the ancients,[15] and most passive chreiai are epideictic in nature.

A passive action chreia may be made into a sayings chreia in which

---

[15] See D. A. Russell and N. G. Wilson (eds.), *Menander Rhetor* (Oxford: Clarendon, 1981), and Theodore G. Burgess, *Epideictic Literature* (Chicago: University of Chicago, 1902).

the person with the good or bad qualities actively comes to speech. For example, the gospel of Matthew contains the following version of the temptation scene discussed above:

> Then Jesus was led up by the Spirit into the wilderness to be tempted by the devil. And he fasted forty days and forty nights, and afterward he was hungry. And the tempter came and said to him, "If you are the Son of God, command these stones to become loaves of bread." But he answered, "It is written, 'Man shall not live by bread alone, but by every word that proceeds from the mouth of God'." (Mt 4:1–4)[16]

In this instance, the action by the Spirit and the devil upon Jesus occur in the first part, and Jesus' response turns the chreia into an "active" sayings chreia.

Before leaving the classification of the chreia, we need to see an additional item which is shown but not discussed by Theon. Then we will apply what we have seen to a double chreia in the NT before we follow Theon into another dimension of the chreia.

A special challenge for interpreters lies in chreiai which feature a group that speaks with a single voice. Among the chreiai discussed in the *Progymnasmata*, three are attributed to unnamed individuals who represent a particular group. They are:

> A Laconian, when someone asked him where the Lacedaemonians consider the boundaries of their land to be, showed his spear. (Hock-O'Neil 328 [Chreia 45])

> A Laconian, who had become a prisoner of war and was being sold, on being asked by someone what he could do, said, "Be free." (Hock-O'Neil 329 [Chreia 46])

> A Sybarite, on seeing the Lacedaemonians living a life of toil, said he did not wonder that in their wars they do not hesitate to die, for death is better than such a life. (Hock-O'Neil 339 [Chreia 62])

Doxapater cites one chreia which features a group that speaks as a single voice:

> When Philip wrote many threatening letters to the Lacedaemonians, they wrote back to him, "Lacedaemonians to Philip; Dionysius to Corinth; alphabet." (Hock-O'Neil 326 [Chreia 44])

These examples show that while all chreiai are attributed to a person, the person may be an unnamed representative of a group (a Laconian; a

---

[16] The reader will recognize that the Matthean version is then expanded with two more chreiai which make the interchange a three-step contest between Satan and Jesus.

Sybarite) or an entire group (Lacedaemonians) speaking in a single voice. Surely, from Doxapater's perspective, the last chreia is "attributed to Philip." We can see from our earlier discussion that this is a "passive" chreia in which "Lacedaemonians" respond to remarks Philip has made to them in his letters. These observations can help us to interpret chreiai in all Mediterranean literature which contain these brief forms. Let us apply what we have seen thus far to an especially challenging chreia in the NT.

A double chreia featuring two groups, each which speaks in a single voice, occurs in Mt 9:32–34:

> As they were going away, behold, a demonized, dumb man was brought to him [Jesus]. And when the demon had been cast out, the dumb man spoke; and the crowds marveled, saying, "Never was anything like this seen in Israel." But the Pharisees said, "He casts out demons by the prince of demons."

This is a passive chreia attributed to Jesus. Thus, any action by Jesus is in the situation rather than the response. While Jesus and his disciples are going away, people bring a demonized, dumb man to Jesus. Then "When the demon was cast out, the dumb man spoke." The description is put in passive voice concerning the demon and active voice concerning the dumb man. Then the crowds say, "Never was anything like this seen in Israel." This is a statement by the crowds "upon" Jesus. Therefore, Jesus has a "passive" role, receiving praise for his action in the situation. Secondly, however, the Pharisees censure Jesus' action: "He casts out demons by the prince of demons." Jesus remains in a passive role, and the chreia ends with two groups, each speaking with a single voice. As they speak, they juxtapose praise with censure, and thus juxtaposition is natural in a "double" chreia. In the active example concerning Alexander and Diogenes cited above, Alexander censured Diogenes and Diogenes praised himself. In an active double chreia cited by the Vatican Grammarian, however, the second speaker meets censure with reciprocal censure:

> Antisthenes, the Cynic philosopher, when he was washing greens and noticed Aristippus, the Cyrenaic philosopher, walking with Dionysius, the Sicilian tyrant, said, "Aristippus, if you were content with these greens, you would not be dogging the footsteps of a king." To him Aristippus replied, "Well, if you could converse profitably with a king, you would not be content with them." (Hock-O'Neil 306 [Chreia 9])

In chreiai, therefore, people who are passive in an action version may be active in a sayings version, a person may remain passive as two people or groups engage in praise or censure of him or her, or two people may engage in praise or censure of one another or themselves.

The classification of chreiai on the basis of speech and action helps us to move beyond limited understandings of the chreia in the past. The well-known biblical scholar Martin Dibelius mentioned the chreia in the first edition of his study of the stories and sayings in the synoptic gospels but rejected its relation to units in the gospels. He considered the chreia to function only in and through the biographies of philosophers, Greek stories which emerge from the passion for invention, the interest in individuals, and the use of artistic or aesthetic dimensions.[17] When Dibelius included a section on the chreia in his second edition (1933),[18] he considered the entire concentration in the chreia to be on the saying (in accord with K. Horna's understanding of the chreia and Bultmann's understanding of the apophthegma).[19] He systematically rejected the similarities between the chreia and units in the gospels, specifying differences in the nature of the tradition, the content, the character of the subject, the goal of the stories, and the concentration on speech itself.[20] This form of analysis is typical of comparative analysis of early Christianity during the first half of the twentieth century that emphasized differences at the expense of similarities.[21] But other scholars began to open the way for a comprehensive use of both the similarities and the differences. Instead of over-emphasizing the concentration on the saying in the chreia, K. von Fritz (1935) observed that the chreia need not always be in a statement but, as he said it, also could exist in an apophthegm or narrative of an action.[22] Also, he observed that the saying in the chreia need not be a general maxim (an error made by Dibelius)[23] but can relate to a concrete situation. In fact, as we have seen above, a saying can be simply yes or no. Also, the NT scholar R. O. P. Taylor (1946) saw a wide range of similarities between the chreia and the synoptic units, writing:

> the definition [of the chreia] exactly fits the detachable little stories, of which so much of Mark consists.[24]

---

[17] Martin Dibelius, *Die Formgeschichte des Evangeliums*, 1st ed. (Tübingen: Mohr, 1919) 18.
[18] *Ibid.*, 2nd German ed., 150–64; ET: 152–64.
[19] K. von Fritz, "Gnome," *Real-Encyclopädie der klassischen Altertumswissenschaft*, ed. Pauly-Wissowa, Supplementband 6 (Stuttgart: J. B. Metzlerscher, 1896), cols. 87–88.
[20] Dibelius, ET: 156–59.
[21] Among other reasons, this was driven by a "neo-Orthodox" theology,, see Lynn Poland, "The New Criticism, Neoorthodoxy, and the New Testament, *Journal of Religion* 65 (1985) 459–77.
[22] Fritz, RE, col. 88-9.
[23] Dibelius, ET:152.
[24] R.O.P. Taylor, 76.

By 1946, therefore, NT scholars had the opportunity to use insights from discussion of the chreia in the *Progymnasmata* to guide their analysis and interpretation of units in the gospels.

IV. Describing the Manner of Presentation in Chreiai

Not only Theon's definition and system of classification can be helpful to NT interpreters, but also his description of "the manner of presentation" in chreiai. When Theon describes the manner of presentation, he helps us to observe rhetorical features which gave chreiai their place of prominence within forms of communication in antiquity.

Chreiai may be presented, first of all, Theon writes, "in the manner of a maxim." He gives the following example:

> Bion the sophist used to say that love of money is the mother-city of every evil. (Hock-O'Neil 89 [Chreia 10])

The NT contains the following example:

> After the two days he departed to Galilee, for Jesus himself testified that a prophet has no honor in his own country. (John 4:43-4)

Chreiai may also be "in the manner of an explanation." Theon gives the following:

> Isocrates the rhetor used to advise his students to honor their teachers above their parents, because the latter are the cause only of living, while teachers are the cause of living nobly. (Hock-O'Neil 91 [Chreia 41])

The NT contains the following:

> John answered, "Master, we saw a man casting out demons in your name, and we forbade him, because he does not follow with us." But Jesus said to him, "Do not forbid him; for he that is not against you is for you." (Lk 9:49-50)

Also, chreiai may be presented "with wit." Theon's example is:

> Olympias, on hearing that her son Alexander was proclaiming himself the offspring of Zeus, said, "Won't this fellow stop slandering me to Hera?" (Hock-O'Neil 91 [Chreia 48])

The NT contains the following:

> Then Peter came up and said to him, "Lord, how often shall my brother sin against me, and I forgive him? As many as seven

times?" Jesus said to him, "I do not say to you seven times, but seventy times seven." (Mt 18:21-2)

Another of the disciples said to him, "Lord, let me first go and bury my father." But Jesus said to him, "Follow me, and leave the dead to bury their own dead." (Mt 8:21-2)

They showed Jesus a gold coin and said to him, "Caesar's men demand taxes from us." He said to them, "Give Caesar what belongs to Caesar, give God what belongs to God, and give me what is mine." (GThom 100)

Other chreiai are presented "in the manner of a syllogism." Theon presents:

Diogenes the philosopher, on seeing a youth dressed foppishly, said: "If you are doing this for husbands, you are accursed; if for wives, you are unjust." (Hock-O'Neil 91 [Chreia 27])

Codex Bezae of the Gospel of Luke contains the following example:

Jesus, on seeing someone working on the Sabbath said to him: "Man, if you know what you are doing, you are blessed, but if you do not, you are cursed and a transgressor of the law." (Luke 6:5D)

Some chreiai occur "in the manner of an enthymeme," a form which requires the reader or hearer to make a deduction which has been implied but not stated. Theon gives the following example:

Socrates the philosopher, when a certain student named Apollodorus said to him, "The Athenians have unjustly condemned you to death," said with a laugh, "But did you want them to do it justly?" (Hock-O'Neil 91 [Chreia 58])

In this instance, the reader or hearer must deduce that it is better to be condemned unjustly than justly. Chreiai also may be presented "with an example." Theon gives the following:

Alexander the Macedonian King, on being urged by his friends to amass money, said: "But it didn't help even Croesus." (Hock-O'Neil 91 [Chreia 3])

The NT contains the following:

On a sabbath, while he was going through the grainfields, his disciples plucked and ate some heads of grain, rubbing them in their hands. But some of the Pharisees said, "Why are you doing what is not lawful to do on the sabbath?" And Jesus answered,

> "Have you not read what David did when he was hungry, he and those who were with him: how he entered the house of God, and took and ate the bread of the Presence, which it is not lawful for any but the priests to eat, and also gave it to those with him? And he said to them, "The Son of man is lord of the sabbath." (Lk 6:1–5)

Chreiai also may be presented, Theon writes, "in the manner of a wish":

> Damon the gymnastic teacher whose feet were deformed, when his shoes had been stolen, said: "May they fit the thief." (Hock-O'Neil 91 [Chreia 16])

They also may be presented "in a symbolic manner." Theon gives the following:

> Alexander the Macedonian King, on being asked by someone where he had his treasures, pointed to his friends and said: "In these." (Hock-O'Neil 91-3 [Chreia 4])

The NT contains the following:

> Then his mother and his brothers came to him, but they could not reach him for the crowd. And he was told, "Your mother and your brothers are standing outside, desiring to see you." But he said to them, "My mother and my brothers are those who hear the word of God and do it." (Lk 8:19–21)

Also, according to Theon, chreiai occur "in a figurative manner":

> Plato the philosopher used to say that the offshoots of virtue grow by sweat and toil. (Hock-O'Neil 93 [Chreia 51])

Also, they may occur "with a double entendre":

> Isocrates the rhetor, when a boy was being enrolled with him and when the one who was enrolling him asked what the boy needed, said, "A new tablet and a new stylus" [or: "A tablet and a mind, and a stylus and a mind"]. (Hock-O'Neil 93 [Chreia 42])

Sometimes chreiai are presented "with a change of subject":

> Pyrrhus, the king of Epirus, when some people were debating over wine whether Antigennidas or Satyrus was the better flute-player, said, "In my opinion, Polysperchon is the better general." (Hock-O'Neil 93 [Chreia 53])

Chreiai also may contain a combination of manners of presentation. Theon presents the following, which he considers to be both symbolic and witty:

> Diogenes the Cynic philosopher, on seeing a youth who was the son of an adulterer throwing stones, said: "Stop, boy! You may unwittingly hit your father." (Hock-O'Neil 93 [Chreia 28])

Theon's discussion and examples of the manner of presentation take us yet one step further into the nature of chreiai. Chreiai are rhetorical forms. Thus, they contain identifiable rhetorical features. When the NT scholar Rudolf Bultmann wrote his *History of the Synoptic Tradition* (1921), he observed the presence of rhetorical features like counter-questions containing a metaphor,[25] detailed parable,[26] a demonstration or symbolic act,[27] or a scriptural quotation[28] in controversy dialogues. But he did not use Theon's discussion or any other rhetorician's discussion to aid our understanding of the function of such items in brief units attributed to John the Baptist, Jesus, and the disciples in the NT gospels.

V. Composing Chreiai

While the manner of presentation shows us rhetorical features in chreiai, the exercises with the chreia show us how chreiai were composed in different lengths and forms so they could function in a variety of settings of discourse. In order to understand this aspect of the chreia, it may help if we get a glimpse of the use of chreiai in the setting of education in antiquity. Theon tells teachers to find chreiai (and other forms like fables, maxims, and short narratives) in the standard literature of the time and to use them in the education of their students. The literature from which they were to glean these forms included the writings of the philosopher Plato, the historians Herodotus, Xenophon, and Thucydides, and the orator Demosthenes (Theon book II). Why would any one recommend the use of units like this? On the one hand, the ancients considered any time spent with sayings and actions attributed to persons to be well-spent. Theon says:

> the exercise with the chreia produces . . . a virtuous character, since we do this exercise with the sayings of the sages. (Butts I, 40–42)

---

[25] Bultmann, ET:42.
[26] Ibid., ET:42–5.
[27] Ibid., ET:44–5.
[28] Ibid., ET:45.

On the other hand, the purpose was to nurture skills which would make it possible for people to speak correctly and persuasively. As Theon says:

> That these exercises are certainly beneficial also to those who take up the rhetorical craft is in no way obscure. . . . Whenever someone can refute or confirm these speech forms, he is not far behind those who deliver speeches, since everything we do in forensic speeches is in this exercise as well. (Butts I, 25–33)

Activity with these forms was considered an initial stage of preparation for writing and presenting speeches. The student was asked to perform eight written exercises with the chreia to achieve these skills:

1) Recitation: Write the chreia with clarity on the basis of the teacher's presentation of it.

2) Inflection: Write the chreia in singular, plural, and dual numbers; and write it in nominative, genitive, dative, accusative, and vocative cases.

3) Comment: Append a statement to the chreia asserting its nature as true, noble, advantageous, or consonent with the opinion of others.

4) Objection: Append a statement to the chreia asserting its nature as false, base, injurious, or unacceptable by most.

5) Expansion: Compose a longer form of the chreia, enlarging upon the questions, responses, acts and experiences in it.

6) Condensation: Compose the chreia in an abbreviated form.

7) Refutation: Argue the unacceptability of the chreia on the grounds that it is obscure, pleonastic, elliptical, impossible, implausible, false, harmful, useless, or shameful.

8) Confirmation: Write a short essay, complete with introduction, "narration" of the chreia, arguments, even elaboration, digressions, and character delineation, if need be.[29]

The reader may see that many kinds of skills would be attained if he or she performed all eight exercies on a significant number of chreiai. Also, the process would be demanding. Beyond this, however, we need to see that these exercises teach a person to develop argumentative features in and around chreiai. To learn how to be concise, Theon presents the following chreia:

> Epameinondas, as he was dying childless, said to his friends: "I have left two daughters—the victory at Leuctra and the one at Mantineia." (Hock-O'Neil 101 [Chreia 37])

But then Theon presents an expanded form of this chreia, and the expanded version contains rhetorical features he discussed in "the man-

---

[29] Adapted from Hock-O'Neil 95–105.

ner of presentation" and rhetorical features we regularly see in speeches. If we present this version with headings that show us the manner of presentation and the parts of a speech, we get something like this:

A. Praise of Epameinondas through Description
   Epameinondas the Theban general was, of course, a good man in time of peace, and when war against the Lacedaemonians came to his country, he displayed many outstanding deeds of great courage. As a Boeotarch at Leuctra, he triumphed over the enemy, and while campaigning and fighting for his country, he died at Mantineia. While he was dying of his wounds and his friends were lamenting, among other things, that he was dying childless,
B. Response
   (1) Introduction with emotion
       he smiled and said:
   (2) Exhortation with direct address:
       "Stop weeping, friends,
   (3) Explanation
       (a) Statement in a figurative manner: "for I have left you two immortal daughters,"
       (b) Restatement in a non-figurative manner: "two victories of your country over the Lacedaemonians,"
       (c) Conclusion in a figurative manner: "the one at Leuctra, who is the older, and the younger, who is just now being born at Mantineia."[30]

An example of expansion in the NT can be seen in the account of Jesus and the children. A concise version occurs in Mt 19:13–15:

> Then children were brought to him [Jesus] that he might lay his hands on them and pray. The disciples rebuked the people; but Jesus said, "Let the children come to me, and do not hinder them; for to such belongs the kingdom of heaven." And he laid his hands on them and went away."

This is a chreia in which the saying arises as a response to the disciples' rebuking of the people. The manner of presentation of the saying is, in Theon's terms, "with an explanation." In addition, this is a "mixed" chreia, since Jesus responds not only with a saying but also an act of laying his hands on the children. An expanded version exists in Mk 10:13–16. If we outline it as we did Theon's expanded version of the Epameinondas chreia, it looks like this:

---

[30] Based on Hock-O'Neil 101–3.

A. Description of the situation
And they were bringing children to him [Jesus] that he might touch them; and the disciples rebuked them.
B. Response
   (1) Introduction with emotion
       But when Jesus saw it, he was indignant and said:
   (2) Exhortation
       "Let the children come to me, do not hinder them."
   (3) Explanation
       "For to such belongs the kingdom of God."
   (4) Restatement in negative terms
       "Truly, I say to you, whoever does not receive the kingdom of God like a child shall not enter it."
   (5) Action
       (a) And he took them in his arms
       (b) Result: and blessed them
       (c) Manner: laying his hands upon them.

This expansion introduces argumentative features within the perceived boundaries of the story itself. As we will see next, however, this simply was the beginning of the process whereby chreiai played a role in developing the skills to give a persuasive speech.

VI. Developing an Argument Through Elaboration

In addition to the exercise of expansion, Theon discusses the addition of a comment asserting the truth of the chreia or an objection asserting its falsity. Also, he discusses exercises called refutation and confirmation. These exercises show us the process whereby a chreia could be used to begin an entire argumentative speech. As Theon wrote:

> We also consider how we should properly arrange each of the arguments. And so we amplify and criticize, and do the other things which at this time it would take too long to discuss. (Butts I, 36–39)

Theon does not show an example of an arrangement of the arguments, but Hermogenes explains it and shows much of it. Hermogenes calls his example an "elaboration" ("working out") of a chreia rather than simply an expansion of it. His example shows us how a chreia can be used to formulate a speech. We will place Hermogenes' headings where we did with the expanded versions of chreiai above (the parentheses are Hermogenes' explanations when he does not actually give an example of how to write a particular part of the exercise):

A. Praise of Isocrates
   Isocrates was wise (and you amplify the subject moderately).
B. The chreia
   Isocrates said that the root of education is bitter, but its fruit is sweet (you are not to express it simply but rather by amplifying the presentation).
C. Rationale ["explanation" in Theon]
   For the most important affairs generally succeed because of toil, and once they have succeeded, they bring pleasure.
D. Statement from the opposite
   For ordinary affairs do not need toil, and they have an outcome that is entirely without pleasure, but serious affairs have the opposite outcome.
E. Argument from analogy
   For just as it is the lot of farmers to reap their fruits after working with the land, so also is it for those working with words.
F. Argument from example
   Demosthenes, after locking himself in a room and toiling long, later reaped his fruits: wreaths and public acclamations.
G. Possibly an argument from citation of an authority
   (For example) Hesiod said: "In front of virtue gods have ordained sweat."
   (And another poet says): "At the price of toil do the gods sell every good to us."
H. Conclusion
   (At the end you are to add an exhortation to the effect that it is necessary to heed the one who has spoken or acted.) (Hock-O'Neil 177 with minor modification)

Research on this arrangement of arguments (Robbins-Mack) has shown that these headings already were being used for the basic sequence of a speech at the beginning of the first century BCE (Rhetorica ad Herennium IV.43.56–44.57). When we look in the NT gospels, we see a range of partial to virtually complete representatives of this kind of argumentation. For example, we see a partial occurrence of the arguments in the Markan version of the Stranger as Exorcist (Mk 9:38–40):

A. Description of the situation
   John said to him [Jesus], "Teacher, we saw a man casting out demons in your name, and we forbade him, because he was not following us."
B. Exhortation
   But Jesus said, "Do not forbid him."
C. Rationale
   "For no one who does a mighty work in my name will be able soon after to speak evil of me."

D. Statement from the opposite
   "For he that is not against us is for us."
E. Authoritative conclusion with an example
   For truly, I say to you, whoever gives you a cup of water to drink because you bear the name of Christ, will by no means lose his reward.

In turn, the Matthean version of Plucking Grain on the Sabbath (Mt 12:1–8) has an almost complete manifestation of the sequence of argumentation:

A. Description of the situation
   At that time Jesus went through the grainfields on the sabbath; his disciples were hungry, and they began to pluck heads of grain and to eat. But when the Pharisees saw it, they said to him, "Look, your disciples are doing what is not lawful to do on the sabbath."
B. Argument from example
   He said to them, "Have you not read what David did, when he was hungry, and those who were with him; how he entered the house of God and ate the bread of the Presence, which it was not lawful for him to eat nor for those who were with him, but only for the priests?"
C. Argument from analogy
   "Or have you not read in the law how on the sabbath the priests in the temple profane the sabbath, and are guiltless?
D. Argument from comparison
   I tell you, something greater than the temple is here.
E. Argument from the opposite based on citation of an authority
   And if you had known what this means, 'I desire mercy, and not sacrifice,' you would not have condemned the guiltless.
F. Rationale
   For the Son of man is lord of the sabbath." (Mt 12:1–8)

A recent analysis of the Matthean version of the Beelzebul controversy (Mt 12:22–37) shows that this is a chreia refutation which features a highly sophisticated sequence of argumentation.[31] In fact, the analysis shows that even a more intricate form of rhetorical discussion concerning "rhetorical stasis" is helpful to understand the dynamics of the interchange.

VII. Conclusion

It should be obvious, then, that investigation of the chreia, as discussed and shown to us in the *Progymnasmata* and as shown through actual instances in ancient literature, can help us to understand another

---

[31] Robbins-Mack, forthcoming.

dimension of the Christian message in Mediterranean society. The brief stories and sayings which Christians used both in speech and writing to communicate their commitment to God's activity through the prophets, John the Baptist, Jesus, and the disciples were a powerful and natural form of communication in Mediterranean culture. Moreover, much of the debate about the literary or non-literary nature of the NT gospels becomes less important when we see how these forms were at home in both oral and written speech, and were a natural bridge between the two. Brief written forms were presented orally by teachers and orators, and students and others wrote them down (probably saying them aloud as they wrote).[32] Then people worked these brief units up into speeches which they presented orally. The sermon, then, was not the only speech-form in earliest Christianity. Rather, stories and sayings themselves could be presented in argumentative ways, or they could be the starting point for an entire argumentative speech.

VIII. Annotated Bibliography

The best single book on the chreia is Ronald F. Hock and Edward N. O'Neil (ed.), *The Chreia in Ancient Rhetoric. Vol. 1. The Progymnasmata* (Texts and Translations 27; Atlanta: Scholars Press, 1986). For an English translation of all of Theon's *Progymnasmata*, see James R. Butts, *The Progymnasmata of Theon: A New Text with Translation and Commentary* (Ph.D. dissertation; Claremont: Claremont Graduate School, 1986). The most extensive interpretation of NT Gospel passages using insights from analysis of the chreia is Vernon K. Robbins and Burton L. Mack, *Rhetoric in the Gospels: Argumentation in Narrative Elaboration* (Foundations and Facets; Philadelphia: Fortress, 1987). The chreiai in Q are exhibited and discussed in John S. Kloppenborg, *The Formation of Q: Trajectories in Ancient Wisdom Collections*. (Philadelphia: Fortress, 1987). Additional analyses are available in Vernon K. Robbins, "Pronouncement Stories and Jesus' Blessing of the Children: A Rhetorical Approach," *Semeia* 29 (1983) 43–74 and Burton L. Mack, "Decoding the Scriptures: Philo and the Rules of Rhetoric," *Studia Philonica* forthcoming.

Prior to recent interest, the usefulness of the chreia for analysis of the gospels was explored in R.O.P. Taylor, *The Groundwork of the Gospels* (Oxford: Basil Blackwell, 1946) and William R. Farmer, "Notes on a Literary and Form-Critical Analysis of Some of the Synoptic Material Peculiar to Luke," *NTS* 8 (1961–62) 301–316. The term chria came into vogue, however, through the study by Henry A. Fischel, "Studies in Cynicism and the Ancient Near East: The Transformation of a Chria," in J. Neusner (ed.), *Religions in Antiquity: Essays in Memory of E.R.*

---

[32] Bonner, 254.

Goodenough. (Leiden: Brill, 1968) 372–411. An earlier discussion which was available to all NT interpreters but which overemphasized the role of the saying in the chreia is Martin Dibelius, *From Tradition to Gospel* (New York: Scribners, 1934) 152–64.

For a basic presentation of the usefulness of classical rhetoric for interpretation of the NT, see George A. Kennedy, *New Testament Interpretation through Rhetorical Criticism* (Chapel Hill and London: University of North Carolina Press, 1984). On the educational setting in which exercises were performed with the chreia, and for extensive bibliography, see Stanley F. Bonner, *Education in Ancient Rome: From the Elder Cato to the Younger Pliny* (Berkeley & Los Angeles: University of California Press, 1977) 250–76, 380–92 and Donald L. Clark, *Rhetoric in Greco-Roman Education* (New York: Columbia University Press, 1957) 177–212, 266–76. Also, see F.H. Colson, "Quintilian 1.9 and the 'Chreia' in Ancient Education." *Classical Review* 35 (1921) 150–54.

For a discussion of epideictic rhetoric, see D. A. Russell and N. G. Wilson (eds.), *Menander Rhetor* (Oxford: Clarendon, 1981) and Theodore C. Burgess, *Epideictic Literature* (Chicago: University of Chicago, 1902). For additional information about classical rhetoric, see George A. Kennedy, *The Art of Persuasion in Greece* (Princeton: Princeton University Press, 1963); *The Art of Rhetoric in the Roman World* (Princeton: Princeton University Press, 1972); *Classical Rhetoric and its Christian and Secular Tradition from Ancient to Modern Times* (Chapel Hill: University of North Carolina Press, 1980); *Greek Rhetoric under Christian Emperors* (Princeton: Princeton University Press, 1983).

CHAPTER 2
HOUSEHOLD CODES

David L. Balch
Brite Divinity School
Texas Christian University

I. The Origin of the Form, its Social Function, and Characteristics of Individual Exhortations

A. *Evaluation of the Research on Form and Function*

Early in this century, Martin Dibelius suggested that Colossians 3:18–4:1 slightly Christianized a code borrowed from the Stoics, e.g. from a popular handbook pattern like that of Hierocles. The motivations "as is fitting" (Col 3:18) and "acceptable" (3:20) are typically Stoic and are Christianized by the phrase "in the Lord" (3:20).

Dibelius' doctoral student, Karl Weidinger, suggested that Hellenistic Judaism had already appropriated the ethic with little originality; examples are pseudo-Phocylides, *Maxims* 175–227; Philo, *Apology for the Jews* 7.3; Josephus, *Against Apion* II.189–209. David Schroeder continued the emphasis on Hellenistic Judaism. He analyzed forty-nine Stoic lists of duties, thirty-eight of which are in Epictetus. They are close to the NT pattern, but the *order* of the persons addressed in the NT *Haustafeln* and the fact that the NT codes are addressed to social *classes*, not to individuals, as are the Stoic lists of duties, means that the texts in the Jewish author Philo are better parallels to the NT codes. Further, Philo, *The Decalogue* 165–67 assigns duties to *pairs*, and one member of the pair is to be *subordinate* to the other, a concern alien to the Stoic ethic which values individual self-sufficiency. Hellenistic Judaism developed this code out of the decalogue (Exod 20:12), and in NT authors it is emphasized in opposition to the social actualizing of Gal 3:28 by some Corinthian Christians reflected in 1 Cor 7.

James Crouch agrees with Schroeder that the Stoic influence on the NT codes is minimal; however, the ethic was not developed out of the decalogue. "Two Stoic texts exhibit an interest in reciprocity: Hecaton (in

Seneca, *On Benefits* 2.18.1–2; 3.18.1–2. 3.22.1–2) and Ariston (in Seneca, *Ep.* 94.1-3), but they are exceptions. The Oriental-Jewish background of the form should be emphasized; social duties in Egypt and Israel in antiquity were understood in reciprocal terms, especially the relationship between rich and poor. This source for reciprocally responsible ethics is reflected in Philo, *The Decalogue* 165–67, but more importantly in *Apology for the Jews* 7.14 and in Josephus, *Against Apion* II.190–219. These two texts and pseudo-Phocylides are panegyrics on Jewish law utilized by Jewish missionaries in an effort to convert Gentiles, which raises the question whether the NT codes have a similar function. From Oriental and Hellenistic Jewish sources, then, this code becomes one aspect of the nomistic tendency in Pauline churches over against Hellenistic religiosity which allowed license in the cults of Dionysus, Isis and Cybele and against the similar emancipation among Christian slaves and women reflected in Gal 3:28.

In the mid-1970s three scholars—Dieter Lührmann, Klaus Thraede and David Balch—independently rejected these hypotheses; the primary source for the form of the code is neither Stoicism nor Oriental or Hellenistic Judaism. Instead, the NT codes are derived from the Hellenistic discussion "concerning household management" *(peri oikonomias)*, especially as outlined by Aristotle, *Politics* I 1253b 1–14. This Aristotelian text outlines relationships between a) three pairs of social classes b) which are related reciprocally, and c) it argues that one social class in each of the three pairs is to "be ruled."

In 1975 Dieter Luehrmann published an article suggesting that the sources for the NT codes are in this literature on "household management, in Xenophon, Aristotle, the three pseudo-Aristotelian *Oikonomika*, Philodemus and Seneca. He finds the three pairs only in Aristotle and Seneca, *Ep.* 94.1–3. He also suggests the intriguing thesis that these codes make a universal claim; because "household management" is an integral aspect of "politics", the NT codes are latently political. Thus it is not surprising that the relationship to the state is ordered in the code in 1 Pet.

A second article in 1980 analyzes both these texts' meaning in the three "phases" of the social-institutional development of early Christianity and in the social history of pre-industrial societies. The codes in Col, Eph and 1 Pet are discontinuous with the first, Pauline phase of Christianity and assume a conscious debate with that earlier phase. They describe the roles of wives and slaves in a relatively conservative way which remains some distance behind actual possibilities in the Greek tradition. In the third phase, seen in the Pastorals, the household codes become congregational codes which reflect awareness of false criticisms of the church by the Roman state.

Klaus Thraede published a long, independent study in 1977 drawing some similar conclusions, which he developed in another article of 1980. Besides Xenophon and Aristotle, he also stresses the Neopythagorean literature (Bryson, Callicratidas, Phintys and Perictione) which attacks the social freedoms and rights propagated by earlier philosophers, e.g. by Plato and the Stoics. Neopythagoreans protest against the easy living of wives as pictured by the Neronian writer Columella. Similarly, Philo represents the status quo in Judaism where wives, children and slaves are discriminated against.

Thraede's 1980 article spells out the meaning of his earlier observations. The household codes take a *partisan* position *(eine Parteinahme)* over against other available options in Hellenistic culture. This position is expressly anti-egalitarian, but supports a mild, more humanitarian idea of authority, which means that it is a conservative position between two extremes, a realistic, humane middle position, a responsible, rational Aristotelian mean *(mesotes)* between unqualified patriarchy and equality[1]. The NT codes assert a domestic order between the egalitarianism of Musonius and Plutarch on the one hand and the unqualified support for authority seen in the Jew Philo and in Neopythagoreans on the other, so the codes are progressively conservative.

In 1981 David Balch published a revised version of a Yale dissertation originally completed in 1974. The first part traces the Greek discussion *peri oikonomias* from Plato and Aristotle through later Middle Platonists and Peripatetics to Stoics, Epicureans, Hellenistic Jews and Neopythagoreans, drawing the conclusion that it was a common, popular discussion in philosophical schools and among rhetoricians. In the first century BCE, Aristotle's structured discussion of "household management" was summarized in a popular handbook by the Stoic Arius Didymus, Augustus Caesar's court philosopher. Similarly, the topic was discussed at the end of the first century CE in Bithynia, i.e. near the place and date of 1 Pet and Col, by the travelling sophist, later Stoic philosopher, Dio Chrysostom. Again, in the fourth century CE Stobaeus, *Anthologium* IV.28, collected texts which for centuries had exemplified certain common *topoi*, including a long chapter "concerning household management."

The structured discussion of the domestic relationships of *three pairs* is found not only in Aristotle, *Politics* I 1253b 1–14 and *Nicomachean Ethics* VIII 1160a 23–1161a 10 and V 1134b 9–18, but also in pseudo-Aristotle, *Magne Moralia* I 1194b 5–28 and in the (pseudo-Aristotelian?) work *Concerning the Association of Husband and Wife*. It is not surprising that Seneca, *Ep.* 89.10–11 knows that such philosophical "economics" is Peripatetic. Seneca himself, arguing against Hecaton, insists on reciprocity in these three relationships, including the relationships of mas-

---

[1] Thraede in *Pietas* 365, 367.

ters and slaves (*On Benefits* 2.18.1–2; 3.18.1–4). The Stoic Ariston rejected concern with these three relationships (see Seneca, *Ep.* 94.1–2), but was opposed by the contemporary Stoic Chrysippus (who is the source of pseudo-Plutarch, *The Education of Children* 7E). Two important occurrences of this Aristotelian topos in late first century BCE Augustan writers have hardly been noticed. In his handbook summary of Peripatetic ethics, Arius Didymus presents these three pairs when outlining the "constitution" *(politeia)*, the proper form of authority, in the house: "the relationship *(koinonias to schema)* to parents to children is monarchic, of husbands to wives aristocratic, of children to one another *(pros allelous)* democratic (II.148, 16–19 Wachsmuth, translated below). This text has a) three pairs, b) a focus on authority in the relationship, here specifically on the kind of authority exercised, and c) reciprocity in the *koinonia* "to each other" *(allelous)*. Unlike the NT household codes, this is not ethical exhortation, but is practical philosophical ethics. Later in the summary, Didymus argues that the patriarch rules this household because his deliberative faculty is superior to those of wives, children and slaves (II.149,5–8 Wachsmuth); these are the same three classes listed in the same order with the same focus on authority found in Colossians. These same three pairs, again with a focus on authority and obedience, occur in Dionysius of Halicarnassus, *Roman Antiquities* II.25.4–5; 26.1.3–4; 27.1 (see below).

The second part of Balch's book argues that the household code in 1 Peter is "apologetic." The primary evidence for this function of such codes was published in 1982 in an article on the "Two Apologetic Encomia" in Dionysius of Halicarnassus and in Josephus. The Greek historian Dionysius lists "slanders" against Rome (*Rom. Ant.* I.89.1–4) and immediately responds to them by presenting the virtuous, laudable *politeia* (to be translated "constitution" or even "culture") of the Romans. Husbands are to rule their wives, and the wives are to be obedient in all things to their husbands (*Rom. Ant.* II.25.4–5). Children are to honor and obey parents in all things (*Rom. Ant.* II.26.1–4); in fact Romulus gave "greater power to the father over his son than to the master over his slaves" (*Rom. Ant.* II.27.1, trans. Cary in *LCL*).

The Jew Josephus uses the same form for a similar apologetic purpose a century later. Responding to typical invectives like those in Tacitus, *Hist.* V.5, Josephus writes: "the woman, says the Law, is in all things inferior to the man. Let her accordingly be submissive . . . for the authority has been given by God to the man" (*Against Apion* II.201, trans. Thackeray in *LCL*). Children are to honor and respect parents or be stoned (*Against Apion* II.206). And slaves receive severe punishments for crimes (*Against Apion* II.215–17). Although "obedience" is not mentioned directly in reference to slaves, it is a primary concern in Josephus' encomium (*Against Apion* II.158, 193, 220, 225, 235, 293). Clearly, Jews needed to convince Greco-Roman critics that they were compliant residents of the Empire. Formally, the household code in Dionysius is a closer parallel to the code in Colossians than are the laws about marriage and children in Josephus which have been cited since Weidinger.

The book *Let Wives be Submissive* makes a twofold case for a similar apologetic function of the household code in 1 Peter: the Romans' previous experience with foreign cults led them to expect sedition and insubordination, and second, several NT codes are explicitly apologetic. First, foreign cults like those devoted to Dionysus, Isis, Yahweh and Christ Jesus were suspect in Greco-Roman society. The Roman experience with the Egyptian Isis cult was formative. Before the battle at Actium, Octavian called on his soldiers "to allow no woman (Cleopatra) to make herself equal to a man" (Dio Cassius, *Rom. Hist.* 50.28.3). Among those who worship Isis, "the wife should enjoy authority over her husband" according to Diodorus Siculus, *Library of History* I.27.1–2. An Isis aretalogy suggests that this is more than Roman paranoia; among her praises are: "You gave women the same power as men" (*Oxyrhynchus Papyrus* 1380, lines 214–16). The Egyptian Isis cult was both perceived to be and indeed was a threat to Roman customs because it interfered with men ruling women at home and in the state as demanded by the Roman "constitution" according to Dionysius of Halirnassus (quoted above).

The texts of several NT codes exhibit this apologetic function. Immediately following the household code in 1 Peter, the author exhorts the readers: "always be prepared to make a defense *(apologia)* to any one who calls you to account for the hope that is in you" (1 Pet 3:15b). These Christians know that others in Greco-Roman society are "speaking against you as wrongdoers" (1 Pet 2:12b). By being subject to the emperor and his governors, they hope "to silence the ignorance of foolish persons," to stop the slanders of their behavior. (Compare Col 4:6; Tit 3:5; 1 Tim 5:14.) The dominant Greco-Roman society exerted powerful pressure on the devotees of the foreign, Egyptian Isis, on the worshippers of the Palestinian Yahweh, and on the disciples of the crucified Christ to conform to the Roman "constitution." This code is found in three rhetoricians who trained Roman governors to enforce the ethic (Dionysius, Arius Didymus, and Seneca)[2], and, correspondingly, *every* household code found in early Christian literature is in a context exhibiting high tension with the Roman state[3].

My interpretation of these household codes as an apologetic response to outsiders' criticisms differs from Thraede's view of them as a rational, philosophical "mean," a view which leads Thraede to misrepresent both the Neopythagorean and the Stoic texts. He overlooks *numerous* texts

[2] Balch, *Wives* 74.
[3] *Ibid.* 80, n. 58.

when he asserts[4] that Neopythagoreans no longer refer to wives governing slaves (see Perictione, *On the Harmony of a Woman* 142, 22–23; 143, 5; 144, 20 and 25; Phintys, *On the Temperance of a Woman* 152, 10; 154, 10–11; Theano, *To Callistona* 197, 25–28 Thesleff). If the wife is prudent and modest, "she will not only benefit her husband, but also her children, her kindred, her slaves, and the whole of her family: (Perictione 144, 24–145, 1 Thesleff). In fact, she may govern more than slaves:

> For, from the possession of these virtues, she will act worthily when she becomes a wife, towards herself, her husband, her children and her household *(oikon)*. Frequently, also, such a woman will act beautifully towards cities, if she happens to rule over cities or nations, as we see is (sometimes) the case in a kingdom. (Perictione 142, 21–143, 1 Thesleff; contrast Aristotle, *Pol.* II 1269b 12–1270a 15.)

True, numerous passages would infuriate ancient or modern egalitarians, the most offensive of which is probably also in Perictione (144, 8–18 Thesleff): the wife is to bear her husband's unfortunate affairs, ignorance, disease, intoxication and adultery, an error granted to husbands but not to wives; she is not to be jealous, but to bear his anger, parsimony, complaints, jealousy, and accusations so that she is prudent, modest and harmonious! But specifically on the question of whether authority is to be harsh or mild, Thraede overlooks texts like the following:

> Since therefore the husband rules over the wife, he either rules with a despotic or with a guardian, or in the last place, with a political power. But he does not rule over her with a despotic power, for he is diligently attentive to her welfare. Nor is his government of her entirely of a guardian nature; for this is itself a part of the communion (between man and wife). It remains therefore that he rules over her with a political power, according to which both the governor and the thing governed establish the common advantage. Hence, also, wedlock is established with a view to the communion of life. (Callicratidas, *On the Happiness of a Household*, 106, 1–10 Thesleff; cp. Aristotle, *NE* VIII 1160b 23–1161a 11).

Moraux[5] suggests that Callicratidas uses critical adjectives of slavery, for excessive possessions lead to "insolence and destruction" (104, 27–105, 4 Thesleff). Further, in these pseudepigraphic works (with fictional authors and audiences), women address women: Theano, the wife or daughter of

---

[4] Thraede, "Aerger" 67.
[5] Paul Moraux, *Le dialogue 'Sur la justice'; a la recherche de l'Aristote perdu* (Louvain: Publications universitaires, 1957) 82–86.

Pythagoras, writes letters to Nicostrate and to Callistona; Melissa writes Cleareta. Perictione, the mother of Plato, writes of the duties of a woman, and Phintys, the daughter of Callicratidas, writes of the temperance of a woman. This might be compared with Stoic-Cynic practice: Musonius taught "That Women Too Should Study Philosophy," (frag. 3), and among the Cynic epistles, there are letters addressed by Crates to Hipparchia which exhort her to leave weaving for philosophy. But we never hear that Musonius actually taught women, nor do the Cynic Epistles have letters written by women, only by men to women. In contrast, several Neopythagorean women are portrayed as engaging in philosophy; they write and exhort other women. Therefore, the Neopythagoreans are a) reactionary with respect to male sexual practices, i.e., temperance is a specifically female virtue. b) Once, apparently, there is criticism of the moral effects of slavery. c) On the question of the exercise of authority, Neopythagorean texts are characteristically a development of Peripatetic thought sometimes "conservative," sometimes "progressive," e.g. women may rule cities. d) And some women are philosophers; they write moral epistles and tractates to other women. Thraede's generalizations need correction: both Stoic-Cynic and Neopythagorean literature are syncretistic. Neither is exclusively patriarchal and reactionary or egalitarian and progressive.

The *Hellenistic* Jews Philo and Josephus, too, basically reflect Platonic and Aristotelian thought about the household; it is incorrect to portray their "Jewish" ideas as more repressive than those of Greek thinkers. (For Philo see e.g. *Spec. leg.* III.137–38; 2.67–69, cited below under I.B.) They emphasize the Greek ideas as foreign, minority sectarian groups in the process of acculturating customarily do, but their domestic and political ideas remain basically Greek.

Thraede's evaluation is more seriously in error regarding the "egalitarianism" of the Roman Stoics and the Middle Platonist Plutarch. Without repeating the evidence discussed twice elsewhere[6], I conclude that Roman Stoics were egalitarian in theory but Aristotelian in practice. Antipater, Musonius and Hierocles each theorize that the wife is similar or equal to her husband, but then each subordinates her to him in practice. Thraede[7] emphasizes Antipater, but this Stoic's work *Concerning Marriage* observes that "life with a wife seems troublesome to some men because of their inability to rule. . . . They do not teach her anything concerning household management" (III.256,2–5 in von Arnim, SVF).

---

[6] See Balch, *Wives*, Appendix V, "Roman Stoics and Plutarch on Equality between Husband and Wife," 143–49 and Balch, "1 Cor 7:32–35 and Stoic Debates about Marriage, Anxiety and Distraction," *JBL* 102 (1983) 429–39, esp. 436–39.
[7] Thraede, "Aerger" 58.

The Neopythagoreans are not consistently to the right, the *Roman* Stoics (including Musonius)[8] not always to the left of the NT household codes on the specific question of husbands' authority over wives within the larger social context of Roman patriarchy. If these texts are the best available to demonstrate a wide spectrum of available philosophical options between egalitarianism on the one hand and support for unqualified patriarchal authority on the other, Thraede's case remains unproved. His use of the term *mesotes* to describe the function of the NT household codes is an illegitimate attempt to read Aristotle's "mean" (see *NE* II and Thomas Aquinas' *Commentary* on it) into Greco-Roman social history. Thraede correctly criticizes the theological *eisegesis* of Wolfgang Schrage, and then himself attempts philosophical *eisegesis*. Thraede's attempt at historical description might be misused to legitimate the post-Pauline employment of these Aristotelian household codes, which would cover up the radical change in early Christian life style that the codes represent, a change which places this "early Catholic" life style in tension both with the Mosaic covenant (e.g. Exod 21:1–6; Deut 15:12–18) and with the Jesus tradition itself (e.g. Mark 10:15, 28–30).

The rational political philosophy discused above (Aristotle, Neopythagoreans, and Stoics) and the question of whether the household codes exhibit a rational "mean" must be distinguished from the discussion of actual social structures and experiences in Roman society. The Jewish and Christian apologists (Josephus and the author of 1 Pet) take us from the primarily philosophical discussion closer to actual social experiences: they perceived critics of Jews and those "blaspheming" Christians to be demanding conformity to Romulus' (Augustus') "constitution" (*politeia*, as outlined by Dionysius of Halicarnassus), including the obedience of three social groups in the household to their superiors in the domestic hierarchy. These apologists were not responding to a wide variety of options in Greco-Roman society, but to the consistent patriarchal pattern seen in Aristotle, Neopythagoreans *and* in Roman Stoics. Epicureans withdrew from this society into social isolation, and Cynics gave a radical critique, although the actual political influence of the latter seems to have been minimal.[9] Aside from some ineffectual protests from within, the more significant social contrasts in this period seem to be those perceived by Augustan writers themselves[10] between

---

[8] Even Musonius assumes that wives "are ruled" (frag. 12; 86,38-88,4 Lutz). See Friedrich Wilhelm, "Die Oeconomica der Neupythagoreer Bryson, Kallikratidas, Periktione, Phintys," *Rheinisches Museum* 70 (1915) 161–223, at pp. 211–12, esp. n. 8: "Der Auffassung, dass der Mann der herrschende Teil sei, bequemt sich Musonius an; vergleich Kallikratidas."

[9] G. J. D. Aalders, *Political Thought in Hellenistic Times* (Amsterdam: Adolf M. Hakkert, 1975) 55–63.

[10] Balch, *Wives* 69–73.

Greco-Roman society and foreign, Egyptian patterns, or between the Greco-Roman household codes and the earlier Jesus movement in Palestine.

Leaving the Balch-Thraede differences, another debate has developed around John Elliott's *Sociological Exegesis of 1 Peter*. Emphasizing the apocalyptic dualism in the letter, Elliott says it focuses on encouraging the "termination of previous associations"[11] with Gentiles, the termination of past familial, social and religious ties. He employs both conflict theory and Bryan Wilson's early sociological theories of alienation to clarify 1 Pet and the function of the household code in that letter.

However, instead of encouraging sectarian isolation, the household code in this letter promotes integration into Greco-Roman society. Whereas the way Elliott employs Wilson's theories of alienation misconstrues the social changes involved, I argue that anthropological theories of "selective acculturation" clarify the social function of the household codes. A receiving culture selectively adapts cultural traits from a donor culture, which sometimes includes "a model of its family life," although "the family configuration is certain to be refracted" by the "filter of traditional and idiosyncratic perception" of the receiving culture.[12] Modern field studies provide analogies to help clarify the adaptation of Greco-Roman models for family life evident in the Jew Josephus and in the Hellenistic Jewish Christian author of 1 Pet. Revised versions of this discussion with Elliott, held originally at a national society meeting in 1983, have now been published in a collection of essays on 1 Pet edited by Charles Talbert.

Franz Laub has a chapter on slaves in household and in congregational codes. Col, Eph and 1 Pet do not show a special interest in super- and subordination, he thinks, but stress specifically Christian motives: *agape* (Col 3:19; Eph 5:21–33) and the equalizing Lordship of Christ (Col 3:24–25; 4:1; Eph 6:9). What is most notable is not the subordination of the slaves, but that they are *addressed* in the codes. Many modern evaluations underestimate the integrating power of the early Christian congregation.[13] These groups are addressed as members of the *ecclesia*, not as members of a household. This integrating power is something entirely new in ancient social history: masters and slaves have the same

---

[11] John H. Elliott, *A Home for the Homeless. A Sociological Exegesis of 1 Peter, Its Situatiion and Strategy* (Philadelphia: Fortress, 1981) 66.

[12] B. J. Siegel, et al, "Acculturation: An Exploratory Formulation," *American Anthropologist* 973–1002, at p. 983. B. J. Siegel, ed., *Acculturation. Critical Abstracts, North America* (Stanford Anthropological Series 2; Stanford: Stanford University, 1955), 87–91, 192–94 abstracts related field studies.

[13] Wayne M. Meeks, *The First Urban Christians. The Social World of the Apostle Paul* (New Haven, Yale University, 1983) 78–79, and 86–94 makes relevant observations.

Lord and judge (Col 3:25b). However, there is a tendency in later codes to identify existing relationships as Christian.

Karl-Heinz Mueller suggests restricting the designation "household code" *(Haustafel)* to Col and Eph since they alone have the Aristotelian structure. This, however, poses two problems: 1) Modern categories would then be narrower than classical Greek terms. The Greek discussion of "household management" did not always or even usually have an Aristotelian structure. 2) Relationships in the "house" were discussed in the context of "city" management. Therefore, the exhortation to be obedient to the emperor and his governors in 1 Pet 2:13 is consistent with the observation that 1 Pet 2:11–3:12 is a *household* code, as is 1 Clem 21.4–9.

Again, Mueller agrees with Thraede that the code takes a partisan position in a general debate in ancient society about the profile of the family and household; the debate is not primarily an inner-Christian one.[14] Following Thraede, Mueller interprets the codes as promoting an advance to a liberalizing, pragmatic, moderate, middle, humane, sensible social-ethical orientation, not as a harsh insistence on authority.[15] Still, a critique of other options in society is not to be found in the codes.[16]

Karl-Heinrich Bieritz and Christoph Kaehler in *TRE* depend much more on Lührmann's model that there are inner-Christian choices, distinct phases in the social development of early Christianity in which households, wives and slaves are evaluated quite differently.

Winsome Munro argues that all the codes were interpolated into the Pauline and Petrine epistles about the time of the Second Jewish War against Rome (CE 132–35). She identifies both stylistic criteria (antithetic parallelism, specialized vocabulary, and the "rambling character" of the ideas) and ideological tendencies (the change from non-hierarchical and charismatic religious experience to acceptance of societal institutions) which distinguish this "trito-Pauline" Pastoral Stratum. Without knowing it, she has actually rediscovered the stylistic characteristics of paraenesis, but Pauline and Petrine churches learned how to write ethical exhortation before CE 132! Regrettably, none of the works on paraenesis by

---

[14] Mueller, "Die Haustafel des Kolosserbriefes," 279 with n. 54. Contrast Lührmann, "Neutestamentliche Haustafeln" 91–97.

[15] Mueller, *art. cit.*, 278–79, 288–90, 292, 304, 307, 314, 317–18. Whereas Thraede's terminology designating the Christian household codes as a "middle" way attempts historical description, Mueller's interpretation (e.g. p. 290) seems to be an attempt to legitimate these codes over against Schüssler Fiorenza's more insightful criticism of the deep changes they brought in the "early catholic" church.

[16] *Ibid.*, 295, 297. Contrast Balch, "Early Christian Criticism of Patriarchal Authority (1 Pet 2:11–3:12)."

Kamlah, Malherbe, Merk, Nieder, Thyen, Vetschera, Voegtle, Wendland, or Wibbing, and only the works on household codes by Dibelius and Schrage are in her bibliography.

Elisabeth Schüssler Fiorenza published her book in 1984, an insightful evaluation and development of the discussion. Western misogynism has its root in the rules for the household as the model for the state. These injunctions of men express the interests of the owner and patron class. Whereas women had important leadership roles in the early Jesus movement and in Pauline Christianity, the household codes restrict this activity so that outsiders will not take offense. The Pastorals both stratify the church according to age and gender and merge the leadership of wealthy patrons with that of local male bishops which patriarchalizes church order according to the model of the wealthy Greco-Roman household. This restructuring leads to the exploitation of slaves,[17] the marginalization of women and the genderization of ecclesial office within the church community.

Peter Fiedler has just written a comprehensive summary article concluding that "one can certainly recognize influences from ancient discussions of 'household management,' which, however, was closely connected to popular as well as to philosophically modified ethics; the impact of Biblical and especially wisdom paraenesis was guaranteed by the mediation of Hellenistic Judaism, which had itself accepted an admixture of Hellenistic 'household management.'"[18] He then notices the sudden disappearance of this household code from early Christian tests; sections of it are cited after Polycarp, but hardly ever the whole form.[19]

In summary, during the last decade a new theory of the origin of the form of the NT household codes, that their form is derived from the Hellenistic discussions of "household management," has both been proposed and become a consensus. Radical differences of opinion remain. First, do the codes represent partisanship for one philosophical option among many in Greco-Roman society for ordering household relationships (Thraede)? Or do they represent the church's apologetic response to Greco-Roman social, political pressure to conform to a relatively uniform, hierarchical, patriarchal Roman "constitution" (Balch)? Second, are they to be described as an "advance" *(Fortschritt)* over alternatives available in Jewish and Neopythagorean circles (Thraede, Mueller)? Or do they deprive women of prominent leadership

---

[17] See Eduard Schweizer, "Die Weltlichkeit des Neuen Testaments: die Haustafeln," in *Beiträge zur altestamentliche Theologie. Festschrift Walter Zimmerli*, ed. H. Donner et al, 379–413 (Götttingen: Vandenhoeck and Ruprecht, 1977), esp. 407–12.

[18] Peter Fiedler, "Haustafel," *RAC* 13 (1986) 1063–73, at col. 1070 (my trans.).

[19] *Ibid.*, 1074.

roles formerly held in Pauline Christianity so that the codes function to patriarchalize church office and to marginalize influential women (Schüssler Fiorenza)? Third, is there no critique of Roman society in these codes (Thraede, Mueller, Schüssler Fiorenza)? Or do 1 Pet and Col correct key Hellenistic values about justice and piety (Balch)? Fourth, does the code in 1 Peter encourage Christians to terminate familial, social and religious ties with pagans (Elliott)? Or does it function to encourage adaptation of Greco-Roman values (I would employ the sociological category of "selective acculturation") over against social patterns in the early Jesus movement and in Pauline Christianity (Lührmann, Balch, Schüssler Fiorenza)?

B. Characteristic Features of the Individual Exhortations

David Verner names the characteristic structure of the individual exhortations a "schema," which he describes as follows:

> The elements of the schema may be outlined as follows: Firstly, there is an address (usually in the plural) to a group of persons representing a certain social station. . . . Secondly, there is an imperative, variously expressed with imperative proper, infinitive or participle. . . . Thirdly, there is an amplification, which is typically expressed as a prepositional phrase, although other forms are used as well, especially the form *me (ou) . . . alla*. . . . Finally, there is a reason clause providing motivation, theological justification, etc., which is typically introduced by *gar, hoti,* or *eidotes hoti* . . . . Clearly, however, the essential elements of the schema are the address to the defined group and the accompanying imperative. . . . Secondarily, the schema is characterized by the fact that the exhortations which belong to it do not appear alone, but in series with other exhortations of the same type.[20]

Verner agrees that the form of the topos "concerning household management" came from sources external to the church, but the "schema" represents "specific inner Christian influences" which "underwent a traceable evolutionary process . . . essentially unparalleled in pagan philosophical or apologetic literature." This development moves from the codes in Col and Eph, which deal exclusively with household relationships, to the codes of Ignatius, *Polycarp,* and Polycarp, *Philippians,* which include exhortations to other groups including church officers, to the code of 1 Timothy, the most fully developed example.

Verner's thesis is doubly problematic. First, the definition of the "schema" is ambiguous at both "essential" points: a) the address may be either direct or indirect, and b) the imperative may be one of several

---

[20] Verner, *The Household of God* 87. The following summarizes Verner 87–106.

grammatical forms. Describing these individual exhortations as conforming to "the schema" obscures important differences. Second, the characterization of the household management topos as an external influence and the "schema" as an internal, Christian development overemphasizes the uniqueness of the latter. There are at least two possible pre-Christian sources for the characteristic features of these individual exhortations: wisdom literature and the Hellenistic diatribe.

Proverbs 1–9 contains exhortations with both essential features, but the direct address is usually to the individual.[21] Prov 1:8, "Hear, son, the instruction of your father, and reject not the rules of your mother." Prov 4:1, "Hear, children, the instruction of a father, and attend to know understanding." This is continued in Sirach where, again, the direct address is usually to individuals.[22] Sirach 2:7–11, "You who fear the Lord (plural articular participle), wait for his mercy. . . . You who fear the Lord, hope for good. . . . Look at the generations of old . . . , for (*dioti*) the Lord is full of compassion."

Closer parallels are found in Hellenistic-Jewish homilies.[23] Direct address to the Jewish congregation is quite rare in these homilies, but some examples include imperatives which are similar to the individual exhortations in the NT household codes. There is direct address with one or more imperatives in the following Philonic texts: *De miqr.* 136–38; *De sacrif.* 32; 70; *De fuqa* 85; *Leg. alleg.* 3.219. Perhaps the most striking is *De sacrif.* 70: "Flee, you fools, . . . and cast away. . . ." 4 Macc 18:1 includes address, imperative and amplification. Philo, *De cherub.* 48–49 includes address, imperative, amplification and reason: "These thoughts, ye initiated, . . . receive and . . . babble not. . . . Rather . . . guard . . . not. . . . But . . . press him closely, cling to him . . . For . . ." (trans. Colson in LCL) Philo, *Quis. rer.* 105–06 and *De somn.* 1.165 also exhibit these elements, giving the theological reason in a *hina* clause. Two important texts in Philo indirectly address slaves (24), and they are quite similar to the indirect address to slaves in the Pastorals. *Spec. leg.* 3.137, "Masters should not make excessive use of their authority over slaves . . . for these are no . . . but. . . ." Even more striking is *Spec. leg.* 2.67–68, which contradicts Verner's assertion that the "schema" is not associated with the household management topos anywhere except in the Christian codes. "The masters must be accustomed to work, not . . . so . . . not . . . but. . . . While on the other hand the servants are not to refuse . . . but should find . . . and look forward. . . . For no man is naturally a

---

[21] Dieter Zeller, *Die Weisheitlichen Mahnsprüche bei den Synoptikern* Würzburg: Echter, 1977, 1983) 32–33, 47.

[22] Zeller, *Mahnsprueche* 38, n. 197 gives exceptions, which are quoted below.

[23] Hartwig Thyen, *Der Stil der Jüdisch-Hellenistischen Homilie* (FRLANT 47; Göttingen: Vandenhoeck and Ruprecht, 1955) 43–44, 88–90, 94–96, 100 gives the texts cited below.

[24] Balch, *Wives* 54.

slave" (trans. Colson in LCL). This text indirectly addresses two social groups related reciprocally, has imperatives, amplification and reasons; it lacks an explicit verbal emphasis on subordination, probably because Philo is discussing freedom on the Sabbath.

Tobit 4:3–21 also exhibits the form of the NT exhortations: address and repeated imperatives with reasons (often *dioti* or *gar*). Tobit instructs his son Tobias about his duties in relationship to his father, mother, God, the poor, a wife (an extended treatment in 4:12–13), hired laborers, himself, the hungry and naked, and finally, about worship.

The elements of the individual exhortations in the NT codes occur dozens of times in the *Testaments of the XII Patriarchs*. Some instances that include address and imperatives in some striking way related to the New Testament codes are: *Test. Reuben* 4:1–2, 5–11; 6:2; *Zebulun* 5:1, 3; *Dan* 5:1, 3; *Gad* 6:1–2; *Joseph* 10:1–3; 11:1–2. The texts in *Test. Joseph* state the possibility that the persons addressed may be slaves; therefore, they are similar to texts quoted above from Philo, *Spec. leg.* and to codes in the Pastorals. Among the dozens of examples of the "schema," I quote *Test. Reuben* 5:5–6. "*Flee*, therefore, fornication, *my children*, and *command* your wives and your daughters, that they adorn not their heads and faces to deceive the mind: *because* every woman who useth these wiles hath been reserved for eternal punishment. *For* thus they allured the Watchers. . . ." (trans. R. H. Charles).

This "schema" is derived from the style of the Hellenistic diatribe, which after a variety of terms of address, begins sentences with "either (a) an inditing rhetorical question, (b) an inditing statement, or (c) an imperative."[25] Some examples Stowers cites are:

> Man, practice *(anthrope, askeson)*, if you are arrogant, to submit when you are reviled, not to be disturbed when you are insulted. (Epictetus, *Dis.* 3.12.10, trans. Oldfather in LCL)

> Whenever a man drinks water only, or has some ascetic practice he takes every opportunity to talk about it to everybody. . . . Man *(anthrope)*, if it is good for you to drink water, drink it *(pine)!* (Epictetus, *Dis.* 3.14.4–5, trans. Oldfather in LCL; cp. Ignatius, *Poly.* 5.2)

The "schema" is not "unparalleled," nor is it simply an internal Christian development.

The direct address in the Stoic texts is usually to the individual wise male, but it becomes a plural address in some of Philo's homilies (*De fuga*

---

[25] Stanley Kent Stowers, *The Diatribe and Paul's Letter to the Romans* (SBLDS 57; Chico: Scholars, 1981) 87; he cites examples at 216, n. 47.

85; *Leg. alleg.* 3.219), even a plural participle (*De sacrif.* 7; *De migr.* 136–38, which uses the pl. part. of *methiemi,* as does *De somn.* 1.165). *Spec. leg.* 3.137 and 2.67–68 address masters and slaves with infinitive constructions. So the Stoic lists of the individual wise man's duties in relationships, where the imperative mood seldom occurs, become plural exhortations in some of Philo's homilies and in Christian exhortations addressed (directly or indirectly) to social classes. But the assumptions of the two are fundamentally different. God sends the individual Cynic (Epictetus, *Dis.* 3.22.23, 46; cp. 2.22.15; 3.24.78; 4.1.101), but the early Christians were irreducibly a community called by God (e.g. Col 1:18; Eph 2:13–14; 1 Pet 1:2; Polycarp, *Phil.* salutation).

Given the examples of the "schema" discussed and quoted above, I argue that it is *possible* that the authors of 1 Peter and/or Colossians combined the (originally Aristotelian) topos and the paraenetic "schema" (related to the style of the diatribe) independently of each other. The Hellenistic Christian authors of these books stand in the paraenetic tradition of Hellenistic Judaism as seen in Tobit 4, the *Testaments* and Philo, and of Roman Stoics as seen in Epictetus and Hierocles. Still, Verner may be correct that some Christian authors were dependent on earlier Christian authors. Thyen observes[26] that there are many possibilities for constructing the grammatical form of paraenesis in homilies, and he has not found a unified picture. Verner has pointed to more striking similarities which occur repeatedly over decades. An assertion David Aune makes[27] in another connection is relevant: "In fact, 'new' genres were constantly emerging during the Graeco-Roman period, if by 'new' we mean a recombination of earlier forms and genres into novel configurations."

Verner comes close to such a conclusion when he compares the exhortations to slaves in 1 Tim 6:1 and Tit 2:9–10. He observes that although the same thought is expressed, the choice of words and concepts is quite different in the two passages, with different rationals for obedience. "It thus appears that what stands behind these two passages is neither a written source nor a fixed tradition, but the traditional station code schema and the traditional notion of the behavior expected of a slave."[28] Since the "schema" is relatively common, not uniquely Christian as he supposes, even the same (?) author plays with the combination of the schema and the topos in different ways. Both the topos and the "schema" were such common forms in Graeco-Roman culture that other

---

[26] Thyen, *Homilie* 100.
[27] David Aune, "The Problem of the Genre of the Gospels: A Critique of C. H. Talbert's *What is a Gospel?*" in *Gospel Perspectives. Studies of History and Tradition in the Four Gospels,* ed. R. T. France and D. Wenham, 9–59 (Sheffield: JSOT, 1981) 48.
[28] Verner, *Household* 102.

Christian preachers and authors might independently have combined earlier forms into novel configurations as the author of the Pastorals has done.

II. Arius Didymus, Concerning "Household Management" and "Politics"

A. Introduction

Arius Didymus, a Stoic, was Augustus Caesar's friend and philosophical teacher (Suetonius, *Augustus* 89.1; Plutarch, *Antony* 80.1; Dio Cassius, *Roman History* 51.16.4). "Arius seems to have actually played the role which Plato dreamed of and Kant recommended: the philosophers as intimate counsellor to a king or emperor."[29] Didymus became imperial procurator in Sicily but declined Augustus' offer to make him the first prefect of Egypt.[30] His son, Nicanor, looked after Augustan interests in Greece.

He wrote an epitome of Aristotle's ethical, political and domestic philosophy. It has been debated whether Arius drew on an early Peripatetic handbook from the third century BCE or whether this handbook summary was influenced by the Stoicism of Antiochus of Ascalon (c. 120 to 68 BCE), and the answer seems to be that there are sources of various dates. For comparison, Henkel[31] supplies both the Aristotelian texts listed to the right of the translation given below and a list of post-Aristotelian ideas and terms. One later ideal is that marriage is a "sharing of life" (*biou koinonia*, II.148,6 Wachsmuth-Hense), an idea found also in the Stoic Musonius (frag. 13A; 88,13 Lutz; also frag. 14; 94,8 Lutz) and in the Neopythagoreans Callicratidas (103,28; 104,17 Thesleff) and Phintys (153,1–2 Thesleff; compare 1 Cor 7:4), a good example of the syncretism of the age. However, Regenbogen denies that this is simply Stoic material; it represents a rethinking from within the Peripatetic system.[32] The text translated below gives the larger political context in which Greco-Roman persons, including Augustus and his governors, Seneca and his brother Gallio, would have understood the household.

---

[29] Charles H. Kahn, "Arius as Doxographer," in *On Stoic and Peripatetic Ethics. The Work of Arius Didymus*, ed. W. W. Fortenbaugh (Rutgers University Studies in Classical Humanities 1; New Brunswick: Transaction, 1983) 6.

[30] G. W. Bowersock, *Augustus and the Greek World* (Oxford: Clarendon, 1965) 38, 40. See Balch, *Wives* 40–43, 74.

[31] Hermann Henkel, "Zur Politik des Aristoteles. Der Abriss der peripatetischen Ökonomik und Politik bei Stobaios und die Politik des Aristoteles," in *Gymnasium zu Seehausen in der Altmark* (Stendal: Franzen und Grosse, 1875) 10–17, at pp. 16–17.

[32] Otto Regenbogen, "Theophrastos," *PWSup* 7 (1940) 1493–94.

Household Codes 41

B. Translation of Arius Didymus[33]

147,26	Having sufficiently defined "virtues" and, more or less, the many crowded headings of the topos on "ethics," it is necessary successively to go through in detail both "household management" and "politics," since the human being is by nature a political animal.	P I.1,9
148,5	A primary kind of association *(politeia)* is the legal union of a man and a woman for begetting children and for sharing life. This is called a household and is the source for a city, concerning	P I.1,4 NE VIII.12,7
148,8	which it is also necessary to speak. For the household is like any small city, if, at least as is intended, the marriage flourishes, and the children mature and are paired with one another; another household is founded, and thus a third	P I.1,7
148,12	and a fourth, and out of these, a village and a city. After many villages come to be, a city is produced. So just as the household yields for the city the seeds of its formation, thus also it yields the constitution *(politeia)*. Connected with the house is a pattern of monarchy, of aristocracy and of democracy. The	P I.1,8
148,16	relationship of parents to children is monarchic, of husbands to wives aristocratic, of children to one another democratic. For the male is to unite with the female in accordance with a desire for begetting children and for continuing the race. For each of the two is to aim at producing children. When they come together and take for	NE VIII.10,4–6 P I.1,4
149,1	themselves a helper of the partnership—	P I.1,16

[33] The section of Arius Didymus translated below is taken from the handbook of Stobaeus, who, in the early fourth century AD, excerpted many authors; this portion of Didymus is in Stobaeus, book II, chapter 7, excerpt number 26. In the margin to the left of the translation, I will give the page and line of the Greek text edited by C. Wachsmuth and O. Hense, *Stobaeus, Anthologium* (Berlin: Weidmann, 1958), vol. II. In the margin to the right of the translation, I will give parallels in Aristotle, *Politics* (=P) and *Nichomachean Ethics* (=NE) pointed out by Henkel.

	either a slave by nature (strong in body for service, but stupid and unable to live by himself, for whom slavery is beneficial) or a slave by law—a household is organized by the union of the ones added together and by the forethought	P I.2,6–7

P I.2,14–16 |
| 149,5 | of all for one thing that is profitable. The man has the rule of this household by nature. For the deliberative faculty in a woman is inferior, in children it does not yet exist, and in the case of slaves, it is completely absent. Economic prudence, which is the controlling both of a household itself and of those things related to | P I.5,6 |
| 149,10 | the household, is naturally fitting for a man. Belonging to this are the arts of fatherhood, marriage, being a master, and money-making. Just as an army needs armament, a city public revenues, and an | P I.5,1
P I.2,1–2

P I.2,4 |
| 149,14 | art its tools, so also a household needs necessary things. These are twofold: those necessary for living ordinary life and those for living well. Of these it is necessary that the householder first have foresight either that the revenues increase through occupations fit for freemen or that expenditures be moderate. For clearly this division of household management is the most important. Therefore the householder must be experienced in farming, sheep herding and mining, in order that he might discern the profit which is at the same time the greatest | P I.4,1–2 |
| 149,21 | and the most just. There is a better and a worse kind of moneymaking. The better kind is engaged in according to nature and the worse through trade. And these things are sufficient concerning "household management." | P I.3,23 |
| 150,1 | "Concerning politics" these might be the headings. First, cities were organized both because the human being is social by nature and because it is useful. | P III.4,2–3

P III.1,8 |
| 150,5 | Next, the most perfect partnership is a city, and a citizen is one who has a claim to civic office. A city is the population composed of enough people for a self- | P I.1,8

P III.1,8 |

Household Codes   43

	sufficient life. The population is	
	limited to the degree that the city is	
	neither unfeeling nor contemptible, but	P VII.4,8
	is equipped both to live without want and	P VII.5,1
	to take care of those who set upon it from	P VII.10,8
150,10	the outside. Now household management,	NE VI.8,3
	lawgiving, politics and making war are	NE I.2,6

various kinds of prudence. Household management, as I said, consists in financial administration both of a house and of the things related to the house. Lawmaking is. . . . (lacuna) Politics is. . . . (lacuna) Making war consists in the theory and financial administration of those things useful for the army.

159,17   Necessarily, either one, a few or all   P III.5,1
persons rule cities. Each of these is   P VI.1,10
either good or bad. It is good when the   P III.4,7
rulers aim at benefitting the public
150,20   and bad when they aim at their personal   P IV.2,4
interest. The bad is a deviation from the
good. Monarchy, then, and aristocracy
and democracy aim at the good, but tyranny,   P III.5,2,4
oligarchy and mob-rule aim at the bad.
The best constitution is some mixture of
151,2   the good forms. But constitutions
change many times for the better or the
worse. In general, the best constitution   P IV.2,1–2
is the one which has been ordered   NE VIII.10,2–3
151,5   according to virtue, the worst according
to vice. Ruling, deliberating and judging   P IV.12,7,10
in democracies is by all or by a faction
or by lot, whereas in oligarchies by
resourceful persons and in aristocracies
by the best persons.
151,9   Seditions in cities occur either   P V.2,1–2
rationally or emotionally. They occur
rationally whenever those with equal rights
are compelled to be unequal, or when those
who are unequal have equality. They occur
emotionally on account of reputation, love
of money, advantage, or ingenuity. Consti-
151,13   tutions are destroyed by two causes, either   P V.3,8
by violence or by fraud. The most stable
are those taking care that the public is
benefited.
151,16   Law courts, senates, assemblies and   P IV.11,1
magistrates are properly defined in

	constitutions. The most common magistrates are: a priesthood for gods, an army generalship, an admiralty, a superintendence of the market, a controller of the gymnasium, a superintendent of women,	P VI.5
151,20	a superintendent of children, an office to administer the police and public buildings and streets, a treasury, a guardianship of the laws, an office of tax collection. Some of these are for cities, others for war, and others for harbors and commerce.	P VI.5,12
151,23	The work of a politician is also to reform a constitution, which appears to be much harder than originally to establish one. and the citizenry distribute among	P IV.1,4 P IV.3,11–14 P VII.7,4–5
152,2	themselves the necessary and the earnest occupations. Artisans, menial laborers, farmers, and commercial traders are necessary for they are underlings to the politicians; but to be fit for every battle and to be able to counsel is more lordly since this involves having charge of virtue	P VII.8,1–6
152,7	and being earnest with respect to the good. Among these the presbyter has chief voice in counsel, and the elder serves the divine, but the young makes war for all. This is the very ancient caste system, first established by Egyptians.	P VII.8,4–6 P IV.3,11–13 P VI.5,10 P VII.9,1
152,11	The politician, no less than others, also establishes the rites of the gods in the most prominent places. Private land is to be arranged so that one part is near the frontiers and the other part near the city	P VII.11,1 P VII.9,7
152,15	in order that, since two allotments are distributed to each citizen, both parts of the land might be within easy sight of each other. It is useful to have common meals ordained by law and to pay earnest attention to the public education of the children. For strength and highest perfection of bodies, neither the youngest	P VII.9,6 P VIII.1,3 VII.14,4,11
152,20	nor the oldest should marry, for both extremes of age produce deformed children, and the offspring are completely weak. It is to be ordained by law that one is to rear no deformed child, nor to expose a whole child, nor to abort a useful child, I presume. And concerning	P VII.14,10 P VII.14,10
152,25	"politics," these are the main headings.	

III. Notes on Arius Didymus' Text

As noted above, when outlining the topos on "household management," Didymus presents the relationships by pairs (II.148,16–19 Wachsmuth), then emphasizes that the patriarch is the ruler over women, children and slaves (II.149,5–8 Wachsmuth). The topos retains its Aristotelian, four-part structure: fatherhood, marriage, mastership, and moneymaking (II.149,10–12 Wachsmuth). Didymus (II.149,17–18) agrees with the Epicurean Philodemus, *Concerning Household Management* (38,5–9 and 17–19 Jensen) that "moneymaking" is the most important topic in this discussion. On the other hand, the pseudo-Aristotelian *Magna Moralia* (I 1194b 5–28) and the NT codes drop this aspect of the discussion (but see 1 Tim 6:6–10, 17–19; Polycarp, *Philippians* 4).

The nature of the authority exercised within these relationships is still a concern (II.148,15–16 Wachsmuth), as it is in Callicratidas (quoted above). Col 3:19, 21; 4:1; Eph 5:25–29, 33; 6:4, 9; 1 Pet 2:20; 3:6; Ignatius, *Poly* 4:3, etc., show a similar concern. The exhortation to masters in Eph 6:9 to "forbear threatening" is similar to Philodemus, *Concerning Household Management* (32,3–7 Jensen): slaves' punishment is to be moderate, not unreasonable.

Didymus' text still relates the house to the city. The NT codes drop this vocabulary, although some exhort Christians to be obedient to rulers of the state (1 Pet 2:13–17; 1 Tim 2:1–2; Tit 3:1; see 1 Clem 21:1; 61:1).

Many, even most, of the basic questions in Aristotle's *Politics* are mentioned in Arius' short epitome! He epitomizes Aristotle's first and seventh books most often, never from the second or eighth. This relatively complete summary of Aristotle's politics assumes the revival of the peripatetic school in 40–20 BCE by Andronicus of Rhodes, who published a new edition of Aristotle's treatises.

Finally, the Greek style is execrable. Didymus uses a significant number of imperatival infinitives, some of which are dependent on words like *anagkaion*, but for most, one must supply something like *legetai*. Blass-Debrunner-Funk #389 observe that this usage in the NT is rare; they cite the accusatives with infinitives in the household code of Tit 2:2–10, with its single *parakalei* in vs. 6. Didymus uses impersonal verbs often: *anagkaion, lekteon, chresimon*.

IV. Household Codes in the New Testament and in Early Christian Literature

Sampley and Verner observe that the Christian household codes go through a clear development.[34] The greatest number of social classes are

---

[34] Sampley, *"And the two shall become one flesh"* 17–27 and Verner, *Household of God* 89–106.

addressed in Col and Eph: six groups in three pairs. In 1 Pet, not all these classes are addressed or even all three pairs. Slaves, not masters, are addressed, and the parents-children pair disappears, although there is a final address to "all of you" (1 Pet 3:8).

In the Pastoral epistles, neither masters nor children are ever addressed. Nor are the pairs of classes as frequent in the Pastorals. The author gives directions for admonishing slaves (1 Tim 6:1-2 and Tit 2:9-10) with no corresponding admonitions for masters. And where the social classes are paired, the attention of one social group is not always directed toward the other, unlike the earlier codes. It is a parallel phenomenon that the reciprocal pronoun, *allelon*, which Paul employs to emphasize mutual relationships, and which is present in the deutero-Pauline books Ephesians and Colossians, virtually disappears in the Pastorals. Most often, these authors clarify how the wife is to relate to the husband (see 1 Tim 2:12-14; 3:4; 6:1-2; Tit 2:4-5; Callicratidas 107,9-11 Thesleff; Perictione 142,22-23 Thesleff; Phintys 152,4-5 Thesleff; Polycarp, *Phil* 4.2). Then in Tit 2:2-6, the social groups of men and women are divided by age, a unique division in the NT codes.

Just as important, the direct address to the various classes prominent in Col, Eph and 1 Pet is entirely absent from the Pastorals, from Ignatius, *Polycarp* and Polycarp, *Philippians*. Ignatius changes the exhortations even more: instead of even indirect address to widows, he makes them the object of care (cp. 1 Tim 5:4). And instead of addressing slaves, he is concerned with the bishop's behavior toward them.

The *address* to *all* these social classes is unusual. Addressing slaves has precedents in the Hellenistic Jew Philo, *Spec. leg.* 2.67-68; 3.137 and in the *Test. of Joseph* 10:1-3; 11:1-2. The address to wives and children is older than Hellenistic Judaism. Two of Aristotle's personal disciples, Aristoxenus and Dicaearchus, wrote of "four speeches" by Pythagoras to different population groups in Croton.[35] The four speeches as given in Iamblichus, *Life of Pythagoras* 35-57, have some sources in these two Peripatetics, were expanded by Timaeus (356-260 BCE), and again by Iamblichus; von Fritz assigns *Life* 37, 42, 54, 56 and 71 to Timaeus, three centuries before Philo. Phythagoras addresses the young (*neaniskoi*), the elders (*presbuteroi*), children, and wives. The young must "willingly obey their parents" (178,29-30 Thesleff). The "fathers" are to try to be loved (*agapasthai*) by their children (180,32-33) and have sexual relations only with their wives (180,34-35). The wives are to "to love the men they have married" (182,26-27) and not to oppose them at all (182,27-28). But more important than the content of these speeches is

---

[35] Kurt von Fritz, *Pythagorean Politics in Southern Italy. An Analysis of the Sources* (New York: Columbia University, 1940) 16, 18, 31, 36-44, 65-66 and J. S. Morrison, "Pythagoras of Samos," *The Classical Quarterly* 50 (1956) 135-36, 143-46, 152.

the fact that in the Aristotelian tradition such social classes were addressed. However, the direct address to *slaves* in Col, Eph and 1 Pet remains quite unusual, an observation which supports aspects of Laub's interpretation.

Leaving aside these "four speeches," the Pastorals are closer to the rest of the Peripatetic-Neopythagorean tradition than is Col. Social groups are paired in Aristotle, but not often in the later Neopythagorean treatises nor in the Pastorals. In both the Peripatetic and Neopythagorean traditions, slaves are the object of care as in Ignatius and Polycarp. In other words, the movement from Col and 1 Pet to the Pastorals is a movement toward what is more common in contemporary Hellenistic household ethics, losing what is most unusual. This development loses the reciprocity reflected a) in the pairing of social classes and b) their being exhorted to relate to each other, and it loses the direct address to slaves, anticipated by Philo, not by the Peripatetics.

The reason clauses supporting the behavior demanded in the imperatives become entire paragraphs; for example, Ephesians 5 expands the section on wives and 1 Peter 2 the section on slaves, while Ignatius Poly 4 supplements with a list of virtues. Some of these expansions give Christological support (Col 3:24; 1 Pet 2:21–25); some refer to the Old Testament (Eph 5:31; 1 Pet 3:5–6).

The expansion of certain sections is also as old as Aristotle; he expands the master-slave section in *Politics* I and the husband-wife section in his work *Concerning the Association of Husband and Wife*,[36] although these are not exhortations. Epictetus, *Dis.* 2.10 expands on how one is to relate to others as a man, citizen, son, brother, counselor, young man, old man, father or smith. The Stoic Hierocles' treatise is composed of such expansions. David Schroeder gave forty-four examples of such lists in his second appendix, which are however addressed to the individual male, not to social classes. I conclude with a quotation from Epicetetus which comes closest to contradicting the last statement; at least one of the three underlined pairs in this quotation does not refer to the same male individual!

> (The work of the philosopher is to maintain) with his associates both the natural and the acquired relationships, those namely of *son, father,* brother, citizen, *husband, wife,* neighbor, fellow traveller, *ruler* and *subject*. (*Dis.* 2.14.8, trans. Oldfather in LCL)

V. Annotated Biblilography

Martin Dibelius, *An die Kolosser, an die Epheser, an Philemon* (HNT; Tübingen: Mohr, 1913) was the source of many ideas in this type

---
[36] Balch, *Wives* 34, 37.

of form criticism and was followed by his student Karl Weidinger, *Die Haustafeln, ein Stück urchristlicher Paraenese* (UNT 14; Leipzig: J. C. Heinrich, 1928). The Stoic Hierocles, cited by Weidinger, is translated in Abraham J. Malherbe, *The Graeco-Roman Moral Tradition and Early Christianity* (Philadelphia: Westminster, 1986) 85–104. Invaluable observations were made by E. G. Selwyn, *The First Epistle of St. Peter* (Grand Rapids: Baker, 1981, first ed. 1946), Essay II, "Formgeschichte and its Application to the Epistle," 363–466.

Two North Americans writing original German dissertations on the form are David Schroeder, *Die Haustafeln in des neuen Testaments (ihre Herkunft und theologischer Sinn)* (Dissertation Hamburg: Mikrokopie, 1959) and James E. Crouch, *The Origin and Intention of the Colossian Haustafel* (FRLANT 109; Göttingen; Vandenhoeck and Ruprecht, 1972). An American dissertation making significant contributions is by J. Paul Sampley, *"'And the two shall become one flesh.' A Study of Traditions in Ephesians 5:21–33* (SNTSMS 16; Cambridge: Cambridge University, 1971).

The three scholars who argue extensively for seeking the origin of the form in literature "concerning household management" are Dieter Lührmann, "Wo man nicht mehr Sklave oder Freier ist. Überlegungen zur Struktur frühchristlicher Gemeinden," *Wort und Dienst* 13 (1975) 53–83, esp. 76–79 and "Neutestamentliche Haustafeln und Antike Ökonomie," *NTS* 27 (1980) 83–97. Klaus Thraede, "Ärger mit der Freiheit. Die Bedeutung von Frauen in Theorie und Praxis der alten Kirche," in G. Scharffenorth and K. Thraede, *"Freunde in Christus werden . . ." Die Beziehung von Mann und Frau als Frage an Theologie und Kirche* (Gelnhausen/Berlin: Burckhardthaus, 1977) 35–182. Thraede, "Frauen im Leben frühchristlicher Gemeinden," *Una Sancta* 32 (1977) 286–99. Thraede, "Zum historischen Hintergrund der 'Haustafeln' des NT," in *Pietas. Festschrift für Bernhard Kötting*, hrsg. E. Dassmann and K. S. Frank, 359–68 (*JAC* Ergänzungsband 8; Münster, Aschendorff, 1980). David L. Balch, *Let Wives be Submissive. The Domestic Code in 1 Peter* (SBLMS 26; Chico: Scholars, 1981). The code has an apologetic function in pagan and Jewish texts according to Balch, "Two Apologetic Encomia: Dionysius on Rome and Josephus on the Jews," *Journal for the Study of Judaism* 13 (1982) 102–22. The contemporary ethical meaning of the code is interpreted in Balch, "Early Christian Criticism of Patriarchal Authority (1 Peter 2:11–3:12)," *Union Seminary Quarterly Reveiw* 39 (1984) 161–73. The debate between John Elliott and Balch about the social experiences reflected in 1 Peter is found in Balch, "Hellenization/Acculturation in 1 Peter," *Perspectives on 1 Peter*, ed. Charles H. Talbert (Macon: Mercer, 1986) 79–101, and Elliott, "1 Peter, its Situation and Strategy: a Discussion with David Balch," 61–78 in the same volume. An examination of Neopythagoreans and the codes will appear in Balch, "Neopythagorean Moralists and the New Testament," in *Aufstieg und Niedergang der RömischenWelt*, ed. H. Temporini and W. Haase (New York: de Gruyter, forthcoming 1987, although submitted in 1975), Teil II, Band 26. These texts are in Holger Thesleff, *The Pythagorean Texts of the Hellenistic Period* (Acta Academiae Aboensis, Ser. A, Humaniora, vol. 30, nr. 1; Abo: Abo Akademi, 1965). I use and modify the old translation by Thomas Taylor, *Political Fragments of Archytas, Charondas, Zaleucus and other Ancient Pythagoreans Preserved by Stobaeus and also Ethical Fragments of Hierocles* (London: C. Whittingham, 1822).

Assuming this discussion and developing it is David C. Verner, *The Household of God. The Social World of the Pastoral Epistles* (SBLDS 71; Chico, Scholars, 1981). On terminology see Hermann von Lips, *Glaube, Gemeinde, Amt: Zum Verständnis der Ordination in den Pastoralbriefen* (FRLANT 122; Göttingen, Vandenhoeck & Ruprecht, 1979) 121–50. The codes in the context of slavery are treated by Franz Laub, *Die Begegnung des frühen Christentums mit der Antiken Sklaverei* (Stuttgart: Katholisches Bibelwerk, 1982).

Thraede's interpretation is repeated by Karl-Hainz Müller, "Die Haustafel des Kolosserbriefes und das antike Frauenthema. Eine kritische Rückschau auf alte Ergebnisse," in *Die Frau im Urchristentum*, ed. G. Dautzenberg et al, 263–319 (Quaestiones Disputatae 95; Freiburg, Herder, 1983).

Winsome Munro, *Authority in Paul and Peter. The Identification of a Pastoral Stratum in the Pauline Corpus and 1 Peter* (SNTSMS 45; Cambridge: Cambridge University, 1983) argues that all these codes were interpolated.

An interpretation stressing development and conflict within early Christianity is given by Elisabeth Schüssler Fiorenza, *In Memory of Her. A Feminist Theological Reconstruction of Christian Origins* (New York: Crossroad, 1983); see also her *Bread not Stone. The Challenge of Feminist Biblical Interpretation* (Boston: Beacon, 1984), esp. chap. 4.

The relationship between the codes in the Pastorals and social-religious roles women have in the Acts of Paul and Thecla is estimated quite differently by Ernst Dassmann, *Der Stachel im Fleisch. Paulus in der frühchristlichen Literatur bis Irenaeus* (Münster: Aschendorff, 1979) and Andreas Lindemann, *Paulus im ältesten Christentum: Das Bild des Apostels und die Rezeption der paulinischen Theologie in der frühchristlichen Literatur bis Marcion*. (BHT 58; Tübingen: Mohr (Siebeck), 1979), on the one hand, and by Dennis Ronald MacDonald, *The Legend and the Apostle. The Battle for Paul in Story and Canon* (Philadelphia: Westminster, 1983) on the other hand.

Michael Gärtner, *Die Familienerziehung in der alten Kirche. Eine Untersuchung über die ersten vier Jahrhunderte des Christentums mit einer Übersetzung und einem Kommentar zu der Schrift des Johannes Chrysostomus über Geltungssucht und Kindererziehung* (Kölner Veröffentlichungen zur Religionsgeschichte 7; Cologne: Böhlau, 1985) 32–38, 54–63 has much material on children, but his critique (pp. 57–61) of the theory of the Aristotelian origin of the form of the early NT household codes ignores the use of the three pairs by Seneca, Arius Didymus and Dionysius of Halicarnassus.

Karl-Heinrich Bieritz and Christoph Kähler, "Haus III," TRE XIV (1985) 478–92 interpret the house in Old and New Testaments as well as in church history and practical theology. Peter Fiedler, "Haustafel," RAC 13 (1986) 1063–73 has summarized the variety of influences resulting in the early Christian household code.

On the function of household congregations in Christianity through Constantine see Hans-Josef Klauch, *Hausgemeinde und Hauskirche im frühen Christentum* (Stuttgarter Bibelstudien 103; Stuttgart: Katholisches Bibelwerk, 1981).

CHAPTER 3

THE ANCIENT JEWISH SYNAGOGUE HOMILY

William Richard Stegner
Garrett-Evangelical Theological Seminary

I. Introduction

While the origins and character of the synagogue homily are debated issues, the earliest evidence is found within the New Testament. For example, the Gospel of Luke tells us that Jesus visited the synagogue at Nazareth, read a passage from the prophet Isaiah, and then commented on that passage (Luke 4:16–21). In addition, Acts 13:15 tells us that there were two readings from the Old Testament—a reading from the law and then a reading from the prophets. After the reading Paul was invited to preach to the congregation. Nevertheless, very little is known about the form or the content of such synagogue sermons. Since portions of the Old Testament were read as a part of the service, scholars speculate that the sermon arose in order to give further instruction in the meaning of the passages that were read. However, scholarly accounts of the history of synagogue preaching have little to say about the period prior to A.D. 200 (Heinemann, 1971b).

The golden age of synagogue preaching was co-extensive with the Amoraic period (ca. A.D. 200–500). Sermons strengthened the faith of people, refuted heretics, instructed people in the demands of the law, and made the Old Testament live by addressing biblical passages to the urgent issues of the day. During this period the great stone synagogues of Galilee were built and the great collections of sermons preached in these synagogues began to be made.

Since the collections of sermons were constantly being edited and supplemented, dating any collection is not easy. For example, the first sermon we will study is ascribed to Rabbi Oshaya who flourished in the generation after A.D. 200. Yet Genesis Rabbah, the great collection of which this is the first sermon, was not finally edited until the sixth century. The Tanchuma, the collection in which our second sermon is located, was edited many years after the sixth century.

While dating individual sermons or the collections themselves is difficult, the significant fact about these collections is that they have been studied over the ages by synagogue preachers for illustrations and inspiration. Nevertheless, the scientific and critical study of these collections did not really begin until the late nineteenth and early twentieth centuries.

In studying the Jewish synagogue homily scholars have found the most common sermon type to be the proem. Indeed, approximately 2,000 proems are found in all the collections of sermons. While a complete definition will be given in the following paragraphs, a proem was a short homily that introduced the Torah reading for the week. Scholars have also found that the proem pattern most clearly reflects the live sermon as it was preached from A.D. 200 until about A.D. 500. While the proem became one of the predominant forms of the Jewish homily in the Amoraic period, a few proems first appear in the literature in the period from A.D. 70 until A.D. 200 (commonly called the Tannaitic period). Although many scholars have studied the proem pattern and its function in the liturgy, perhaps the definitive summary of research was written by Joseph Heinemann (1971a). Much of the following discussion was influenced by Heinemann's work.

In order to see the uniqueness of the proem-sermon it is necessary to understand a few of the elements of synagogue worship in this period. Apparently, a focal point of the service was a reading from the Torah or Law or Pentateuch. (The Torah consisted of the first five books of the Old Testament, Genesis through Deuteronomy, and constituted the first and primary division of the Old Testament or Hebrew Bible.) The reading of a passage from the Torah was followed by a second reading, called *Haftarot* (meaning "completion") from one of the Prophets, or second division of the Hebrew Bible. After the readings of two passages from the Hebrew Bible, a sermon might be preached (see Acts 13:15–16). Sometimes the sermon took the form of an explanation of the reading or readings from the first or second division of the Hebrew Bible as we discover from Luke 4:16–21. However, since the Torah was considered more important than the Prophets, it is likely that most sermons were explanations of the reading from the Torah.

The proem differs from what little we know about the form of a first-century sermon in that it is *not* an explanation of the reading from the Torah or Pentateuchal text. Rather, the characteristic formal element of the proem demands that the preacher begin or open with a verse of the OT from outside the Torah or Pentateuch and end his sermon by quoting the first verse of the assigned lesson for that day from the Torah. Most frequently, the proem begins with a verse from the Writings or third division of the Hebrew Bible. In the proem we are about to analyze, the opening verse is taken from the Book of Proverbs. Occasionally, the proem begins with a verse from one of the prophets.

Why does the preacher begin with some "remote" verse that seemed to have no connection with the Pentateuchal text for the day? The preacher chooses a "remote" verse because he sees some inner connection between that verse and the Pentateuchal text for the day. From the "remote" verse the preacher gives a series of explanations and clarifications that succeed in shedding new light on the Torah reading. After reading the first verse of the Pentateuchal text he concludes the sermon. Moreover, since the congregation already knows the assigned Torah reading for the day, the elements of suspense, drama, and surprise are present. How will the preacher explain the seemingly unrelated "remote" text in order to introduce the assigned reading?

Perhaps the peculiar "upside-down" structure of the proem, which begins with a "remote" verse and only at the end arrives at the first verse of the important weekly reading, has led to the correct explanation of its use within the synagogue service.[1] Older interpreters assumed that proems were simply introductions to the longer sermon which followed, since most proems were so brief. However, the "upside-down" form indicates that proems were designed to *introduce* the Torah reading for the week and were given before the Torah was read. Thus, the order of service in the Palestinian synagogue from about A.D. 200 until about A.D. 500 was first the proem, then the reading from the Torah, and, finally, a reading from the prophets. (Of course, prayers and other elements of worship were also included.) Furthermore, since proems ordinarily began with a verse from the third division of the Hebrew Bible, all three divisions would be included in a typical Sabbath service. A longer sermon than the proem would be given on festival days and might be delivered on Saturday afternoon.

In examining the relationship between the Jewish homily and the NT, we should now turn our attention to another form of Jewish homily that might be called a comment on the biblical text or explanation of the Torah reading of the day. H.L. Strack (see annotated bibliography) has called the form an "exposition of the first verses of the Pentateuchal section." Since the formal characteristics were not so rigidly fixed as those of the proem, they will be described in the introduction to the sermon in section III. Here, however, it is necessary to describe the collection from which the sermon is taken and the pattern in which it is set.

---

[1] J. Heinemann, "The Proem in the Aggadic Midrashim: A Form-Critical Study," *Studies in Aggadah and Folk-Literature: Scripta Hierosolymitana XXII* (Jerusalem: Magnes Press, 1971), 100–22, esp. p. 109.

The collection of sermons from which the second sermon we are about to read has been taken is called the Tanchuma. The Tanchuma is a late compilation of earlier materials and the sermons in the collection have been called "literary" sermons in the sense that they were never preached in their present form or arrangement. The literary nature of the sermons is betrayed by the pattern in which they are now found. The pattern usually starts with a "halakic beginning" or question about some point of observance of the Jewish law. The question is introduced by the formula *yelammedenu rabbenu*, "Let our rabbi teach us" and the answer is given by the formula "Thus our rabbis taught." For example, the following excerpt is taken from the Tanchuma, *parasha Noah,* 13, p. 47 of the Buber edition.

> Let our rabbi teach us, a house in which they place an *erub* (*ʿêrûb*). What is necessary for the *erub?* Thus our rabbis taught. . . .

(An *erub* is the placing of a dish so that several houses are regarded as one house and thereby the legal distance a person can carry objects on the Sabbath is increased.)

The "halakic beginning" is followed by "several proems, exposition of the first verses of the Pentateuchal section, messianic conclusion," which contrasts the tribulation of the present evil age with the good time in "the world to come."[2] In this pattern a series of proems again and again introduce the first verse of the Pentateuchal section. Since the use of more than one proem to introduce the text of the day was highly unlikely, these sermons do not represent actual sermons that were preached before an audience. Also, since the "halakic beginning" of the *yelammedenu rabbenu* type fulfilled much the same function as the proem, these two sermon-types were probably not used simultaneously (Heinemann, 1971b).

Thus these literary homilies were often created by later editors who assembled parts from earlier sermons that were actually preached. The sermon in section III has been taken from the larger artificial sermon and explains a specific Torah reading that begins with Gen 9:20.

The Tanchuma has not yet been translated into English. An excerpt from the sermon that has been translated in section III does appear in Ginsberg's *The Legends of the Jews* (see annotated bibliography). Apparently, no complete English translation and no analysis of the form of the sermon that appears below have been published before.

In contrast to the proem, not much research has been directed to the sermon type or formal characteristics (such as introduction, conclusion,

---

[2] H. Strack, *Introduction to the Talmud and Midrash* (New York: Meridan Books, 1959), 212.

main body) of the sermons recorded in the NT. While great interest was focused on the sermons in Acts, this interest was concerned with the theological content of the sermons. The sermons were thought to be summaries of the earliest Christian proclamation. Other scholars, however, held that the sermons were the creations of the author of Acts on the basis of what he thought might have been said or even should have been said on such occasions. Only a few scholars tried to match the formal characteristics of the sermons with later Jewish types, primarily the proem.

The pioneering work of Peder Borgen was a serious study of the pattern of formal characteristics of a NT sermon. Borgen analysed the structure of John 6:31–68 and compared it with passages in the contemporary Jewish author Philo, who wrote in Greek for the large Alexandrian Jewish community, and with two passages in Paul (Rom 4:1–22; Gal 3:6–29). Borgen found that Philo, Paul, and the author of the Gospel of John all shared the same homiletical pattern, although they wrote independently of each other. Thereby he claims to have isolated a first-century Jewish homilectical pattern that is also found in the later collections of sermons.

We have followed the work of Peder Borgen in comparing the homiletical pattern from the Gospel of John with that from that much later collection called the Tanchuma.

II. A Proem Homily of Rabbi Oshaya

A. *Introduction*

The form of the proem reveals that its setting was the synagogue. Recently, archaeologists have uncovered and reconstructed several large stone Galilean synagogues which could accommodate hundreds of worshippers. A popular rabbi would attract large crowds both by his rhetorical skills and by his ability to make Scripture live. The preacher might change the intonation of his voice, "play" with key words from his initial text, dramatize stories from the Bible and contemporary life, etc. The popularity of Jewish preaching has been compared to the popularity of the theater and the arena of the time. Rabbis held their audiences and the sermon became a community happening.

The well-known proem we are about to read has been ascribed to Oshaya or Hoshaya who flourished in the generation immediately after A.D. 200. It is found in a collection of sermons that were originally preached in Palestinean synagogues. Collections of sermons fall into two categories: those that were based on readings for special occasions, such as Passover and other holidays and those that explored the weekly reading of the Torah. The sermon we are about to read falls into the latter category and comes from a collection called Genesis Rabbah because the sermons explain many of the passages in the Book of Genesis. The particular Pentateuchal verse with which Oshayah's proem concludes is Genesis 1:1: "In the beginning God created. . . ." Now let us turn to the sermon itself.[3]

B. *Translation*

Rabbi Oshaya began: *Then I was beside him, like a master workman ('āmôn); and I was daily his delight* (Prov 8:30). '*āmôn* means pedagogue; '*āmôn* means covered; '*āmôn* means hidden; and some say '*āmôn* means great. '*āmôn* means pedagogue, even as you read in Scripture: *as a nurse* (or pedagogue) *('āmôn) carries the sucking child* (Num 11:12). '*āmôn* means covered, even as you read in Scripture: *those who were brought up* (or covered) *in purple* (Lam 4:5). '*āmôn* means hidden, even as you read in Scripture: *He had brought up* (or hidden) ("The Midrash understands it to mean that Mordecai concealed her from the public gaze.")[4] *Hadassah* (Esth 2:7). '*āmôn* means great, even as you read in Scripture: *Are you better than nô'-'āmôn* (Nah 3:8)? which the targum translates as: "Are you better than Alexandria the Great, that sat between the rivers?"

Another interpretation: '*āmôn* means workman '*ûmān*. The Torah says 'I was the working tool ('*ûmānût*) of the Holy One. blessed be He.' According to the custom of the world, when a king of flesh and blood builds a palace, he does not build it from his own skill, but from the skill of a workman ('*ûmān*). The workman (also architect) does not build it from his own skill, but he has plans and diagrams for information where he places rooms and doors. So, the Holy One, blessed be He, was looking into Torah and created the world. Torah says: *By means of Torah God created* (Gen 1:1). For *beginning* means Torah, even as you read in Scripture: *The Lord made me* (the) *beginning of His way* (Prov 8:22).

C. *Analysis*

The translation of this text involves several unusual difficulties. The unusual word '*āmôn* involves a wide range of meanings and the preacher

---

[3] While the translation is largely mine, I consulted H. Freedman (*The Midrash Rabbah: Genesis*, vol. 1; London: Soncino Press, 1977) 1. Biblical translations are cited from the RSV except for Gen 1:1. In the discussion following the translation, I drew on notes from Dr. E. Mihaly's lectures at Hebrew Union College.

[4] Freedman, *The Midrash Rabbah: Genesis*, 1, n. 2.

has fully exploited the interpretive element involved in a translation. For example, the preacher interprets ʾāmôn to mean pedagogue, which in the ancient world meant someone who cared for the child and escorted it back and forth to school, while the RSV chooses the more modern term "nurse" in Num 11:12. Lam 4:5 could be translated literally as "covered" or "clad" in purple while RSV uses the more figurative "brought up." In Nah 3:8 the Hebrew term probably designates the Egyptian city Thebes while the Aramaic translation of the Hebrew, which is called a targum, identifies the Hebrew nô with "Alexandria" and ʾāmôn with "the Great."

Since only the consonants were written in Hebrew, the words ʾāmôn and ʾûmān were interchangeable—the vowels "a" and "u" not appearing on the page. The word ʾûmān meant artist or architect and designated a specific kind of workman. Since both ranges of meaning were available to the preacher, he chose ʾûmān for his definitive interpretation. Finally, he translates Gen 1:1 *In the beginning God created* as: By means of Torah God created, for two reasons. First, the preposition "in" can also mean "by means of" in Hebrew. Secondly, Wisdom, who is speaking in both the initial text—Prov 8:30—and in the final text—Prov 8:22—is identified with the word for "beginning" in Prov 8:22. Since the identification of Wisdom with Torah was already made before the birth of Christ, the equation now becomes Wisdom = Torah = beginning!

We have already mentioned above that the Pentateuchal lesson for the day began with Gen 1:1. The proem opens with Prov 8:30 in which Wisdom is speaking. Although everyone knew that Wisdom was God's wisdom, in this verse Wisdom is personified and speaks as if she were an independent entity alongside God. When the proem was written, Wisdom had already equated with Torah for several hundred years (both being feminine nouns) so that here the terms are interchangeable. Thus, in this passage Wisdom/Torah is speaking with God *before* the creation of the world. The new light that Prov 8:30 throws on Gen 1:1 is that pre-existent Torah becomes the architect's plan by which God creates the world.

What is Torah saying in the opening verse? She is saying that she is like an ʾāmôn. Then various possible meanings for the term are listed and in good rabbinic fashion each possible meaning is proved by its usage in other verses from the Hebrew Bible. Thus, Torah claims to be hidden with God and covered up (before she was given to Israel on Mt. Sinai?), nursed, so to speak, by the Almighty.

Torah then comes to the main point in the section labeled "another interpretation." She is the "working tool" or blueprint of the world. God created the world with Torah as His blueprint! Notice how naturally this illustration from everyday life fits into the sermon! The four definitions are left behind and only the final one is important.

Two technical features of rabbinic methodology are found in this proem. Scripture is almost always introduced by a formula as is indicated by the repetition of the clause: "even as you read in Scripture." The other technical feature concerns a rabbinic principle for interpreting Scripture. Thus, what is said about a word or phrase in one passage may be used to shed additional light upon the same word or phrase in another passage. The fact that "beginning" means Torah in Prov 8:22 enables the preacher to define the word "beginning" by means of the word "Torah" in Gen 1:1.

A final observation concerns the form of the proem itself. Most proems end by quoting the first verse or a few words from the first verse of the weekly Torah reading. This one does not. The crucial step in interpretation is given after the quotation from Gen 1:1 in the phrase "For *beginning* means Torah," followed by the proof-text. Apparently, the proem form was still flexible enough to allow exceptions in the generation after A.D. 200.

In answer to the question: how could a sermon be so brief? the answer is that initially it was not. Some sermons were memorized before they were committed to writing and in the process were shortened. They were further abbreviated when they were written; consequently, many proems are simply outlines of the main points of the sermon.

III. The Comment on the Biblical Text: A Homily on Noah

A. Introduction

In exploring the relationship between the Jewish homily and the NT, we should now examine another form of Jewish homily which H. L. Strack called an "exposition of the first verses of the Pentateuchal section." This sermon-type has also been called a comment on the biblical text as well as the body of the sermon.

This sermon-type did not possess a form as fixed as that of a proem. Not all the formal features of an "exposition" or comment on the biblical text are found in every sermon of the genre and some of the formal features in this sermon-type are found in proems and other types of sermons. Accordingly, it seems best to explore the formal features found in the following sermon as well as other sermons of the genre. The features listed below are found in this particular sermon and other sermons of the genre or type.

1. The sermon begins with a statement of the first verse of the passage or several words from the first verse. This seems to be the distinguishing feature of this form.
2. A key word or words are explained and emphasized throughout the sermon.
3. Other words and phrases from the whole passage (not just the initial verse) are explained and repeated in the sermon.

4. Other biblical verses are cited for purposes of illustration or for developing side points, etc.
5. Illustrations are drawn from Scripture or contemporary life.
6. If Scriptural illustrations are used, the biblical story is frequently retold with imaginative additions to the text.
7. In the conclusion a word or words from the opening verse are repeated to indicate the sermon is ended.
8. Frequently, the main thrust of the sermon is summarized in the conclusion.

In discussing the formal elements of this sermon type we should also remember that the following sermon has been translated from the Tanchuma and consequently is a part of a larger "literary" or artificial sermon. Literary sermons were composed or compiled by later editors of sermons that were actually preached. Thus there is evidence that parts of this sermon were added by a later hand as the work of L. Ginzberg shows.

Fortunately, L. Ginzberg (see annotated bibliography) has translated a portion from the sermon we are about to read and commented on it extensively. He notes that the story of Satan's collaboration with Noah is found in different versions in several earlier sources. The order in which the four animals are mentioned differ and in one source a he-goat rather than a lion is mentioned. Thus this well-known illustration may have been inserted by a later editor. A more probable insertion is the section introduced by the formula "the sages said" since its terse, formulaic style in Hebrew stands in marked contrast to the rest of the sermon, and its assertion that all of Noah's activity in the vineyard occurred on the same day does not seem to be shared by the following story.

Nevertheless, while some passages may have been added by a later hand, the sermon, as it stands is relatively coherent in thought.

Since this is a literary sermon and contains excerpts from more than one sermon that was actually preached, it is difficult to reconstruct the life-situation that the original sermon addressed. Nevertheless, Galilee, the center of Jewish life and the place where many of these sermons were preached and collected, was primarily an agricultural center. We may surmise that many Galilean farmers, like the rich fool in Jesus' parable (Luke 12:13–21) became preoccupied with agriculture, with profits, with the fertility of the soil, etc. Primarily from written records, but now increasingly from archaeologial excavations, we know that Galilean olive oil and grain were exported in large quantities and prized in the ancient world. Viticulture was also common. The story about Noah's drunkenness surely was a warning against drunkenness. We are now better able to understand the sermon we are about to read.

B. Translation

The following sermon is my translation of the Buber edition of the Tanchuma, *parasha Noah*, chapter 13. The RSV translation is used whenever possible, but occasionally, as in Gen 9:20, the Hebrew has been translated more literally in order to communicate the thought of the sermon. Gen 9:20 and key words and phrases from the passage that follows 9:20 have been set in italics so the reader may see that the sermon attempts to explain the passage as a whole. "Soil," the key word from Gen 9:20, has also been italicized so that its importance in the sermon is more apparent. Other biblical verses outside the passage following Gen 9:20 have been cited and set in quotes.

"And Noah began (to be) a man of the soil." (Gen. 9:20) As soon as he busied himself with the soil he became profane (as opposed to sacred). Said rabbi Yehudah son of rabbi Shalom, "In the beginning (Noah was) a man righteous and pure, but now (he is) *a man of the soil." "He planted a vineyard."* (Gen 9:20b) After he planted a vineyard, he was called *"a man of the soil."*

Three men busied themselves with the soil and became profane. These were Cain, Noah, Uzziah. Concerning Cain, Scripture says (Gen 4;2) ". . . and Cain (was) a tiller of the soil." What else does Scripture say (Gen 4:12)? ". . . you shall be a fugitive and a wanderer on the earth."

Concerning Noah, Scripture says, *"And Noah began (to be) a man of the soil." "He planted a vineyard,"* and he exposed himself. *"And he drank of the vine. . . ."* (Gen 9:21a)

The sages said, "On that day he planted, on that day it produced fruit, on that day he cut (grapes), on that day he treaded (grapes), on that day he drank, on that day he became drunk, on that day his disgrace was exposed."

Our rabbis of blessed memory said, "When Noah came to plant a vineyard, Satan came and stood before him. Satan said to him, 'What are you planting?' He said to him, 'A vineyard.' Satan said to him, 'What kind of vineyard?' Noah replied, 'Its fruits are sweet, neither too green nor too ripe, and they make from them wine which gladdens hearts, as Scripture says (Ps 104:15) 'and wine to gladden the heart of man.' Satan said to him, 'Come and let the two of us join together in this vineyard.' Noah replied, 'To life!' What did Satan do? He brought a sheep and killed it under the vine. After that he brought a lion and killed it there. Then he brought a pig and killed it and after that he brought an ape and killed it under the vineyard. Their blood dripped into that vineyard which absorbed their blood. Thus Satan hinted that before a man drinks wine, he is as pure as this lamb that knows nothing and as a sheep before her shearers is dumb. When he drinks a normal amount, he is a strong man like a lion and says that there is none like him in the world. After he has drunk too much he becomes like a pig soiled in his own urine and in something else. When he is drunk, he becomes like an ape, standing and dancing and laughing and bringing forth obscenities before everyone and he doesn't know what he is doing. And all this happened to Noah the righteous man. What? (Did all this happen to) Noah the righteous one whose praise the Holy One Blessed Be He proclaimed? What then of the rest of humanity? How much the more (might happen to them)!"

There is more, for Noah cursed his offspring and said, "*Cursed be Canaan:* etc." (Gen 9:25) And Ham because he saw with his eyes the *nakedness* of his father, his eyes became red. And because he *told* (about it) with his mouth, his lips became curled. And because he turned his face, the hair on his head and his beard was singed. And because he did not cover the *nakedness*, he walked naked and his foreskin grew back over his circumcision. According to all the measure of the Holy One Blessed Be He (he received) measure for measure.

Nevertheless, the Holy One Blessed Be He turned and had mercy on him, for his mercy is upon all his creation. The Holy One Blessed Be He said, "Since he sold himself into slavery, let him go out by the eye which saw and by the mouth which told." It is right that he shall go out to freedom by tooth and by eye for Scripture says (Exod 21:26), "When a man strikes the eye of his slave, male or female, and destroys it, he shall let the slave go free for the eye's sake." And further (Exod 21:27), "If he knocks out the tooth of his slave, male or female, he shall let the slave go free for the tooth's sake."

And is it not a matter of light and heavy (that is, as with human affairs, so with God's)?

If (in terms of human affairs) a man's slave, his property and wealth, because he blinded his eye and knocked out his tooth, will go out from slavery to freedom (in this life), then (in terms of God's dealings), those blessed by God, who are His plantation to be glorified, when they die, is it not so much more proper that they will go to freedom from sins, as Scripture says, "in death, he is free"; indeed, they will go out with all 248 parts of the body (in the Resurrection they became whole). The Holy One Blessed Be He said, "In this world through the evil inclination they multiply sins, but in the world to come 'I will take out of your flesh the heart of stone. . . .'" (Ezek 36:26c). Again Scripture says, "And it shall never again be the reliance of the house of Israel, recalling their iniquity, when they turn to them for aid. Then they will know that I am the Lord God." (Ezek 29:16) And Scripture says, "In those days and in that time, says the Lord, iniquity shall be sought in Israel, and there shall be none. . . ." (Jer 50:20)

Concerning Uzziah, Scripture says, "for he loved the *soil*." (II Chron 26:10) For he was king, and he busied himself with the *soil* and he did not busy himself with Torah. one day he entered the house of study and said to the rabbis, "With what are you preoccupied?" They said to him, (Num 1:51) "And if anyone else (that is, a lay person) comes near, he shall be put to death." Uzziah said to them, "The Holy One Blessed Be He is a King and I am a king, it is proper for a king to serve a King and to offer incense in his presence." Then, he "entered the temple of the Lord to burn incense on the altar of incense." (II Chron 26:16) "But Azariah the priest went in after him, with eighty priests of the Lord who were men of valor." (II Chron 26:17) And all of them were young priests. "And (they) said to him, 'It is not for you, Uzziah, to burn incense to the Lord, but for the priests the sons of Aaron, who are consecrated to burn incense. Go out of the sanctuary; for you have done wrong. . . .'" (II Chron 26:18) And for this he became angry. "Then Uzziah was angry. Now he had a censer in his hand to burn incense, and when he became angry with the priests leprosy broke out on his forehead. . . ." (26:19) And at the same time the hall was split open this way and the other way twelve upon twelve mil (more than half a mile). "And they thrust him out quickly, and he himself hastened to go out, because the Lord had smitten him." (II Chron 26:20b) Who caused this to happen to him? He neglected the Torah and busied himself with the *soil!* (Tanchuma [Buber] *parasha Noah*, chapter 13)

C. Analysis

Now let us examine how the sermon exemplifies the above formal features. (See A. Introduction)

The sermon is a comment on a passage of Scripture which begins with Gen 9:20. Characteristically, the sermon begins with several words from Gen 9:20: "And Noah began to be a man of the soil (*ʾadāmâh* in Hebrew)."

The key word in the text is the word for soil or ground as its repetition in the sermon shows. Moreover, in this sermon this word dictates the choice of the two illustrations. Thus, in the Hebrew text, the word "soil" is found in both passages used for illustration: hence, the word "soil" is associated both with Cain and with Uzziah, as well as with Noah.

The word for soil performs another key function in the literary structure of this sermon. While it is the key word in the initial text, it is also the last word at the end of the sermon. Thus it forms an inclusion or *inclusio* whereby the end is tied to the beginning. As in some modern sermons, there is a correspondence between the opening and closing of the sermon. Also, the last line is the "punch" line that beautifully summarizes the message and ties the whole together.

However, the reader should not lose sight of the basic structure of the sermon by focusing exclusively on the key word "soil." Rather, the

The Ancient Jewish Synagogue Homily   63

sermon is an "exposition" or explanation of the whole passage that begins with Gen 9:20. Thus, the sermon becomes a running comment on the passage with the addition of the two illustrations of Cain and Uzziah and of several applications to the life of the audience. For example, while the story of Noah's drunkenness is a masterpiece of the storyteller's art in its balance and evocative use of animal imagery, structurally the story illustrates the phrases: "He planted a vineyard; and he drank of the wine" (Gen 9:20b and 21a).

Then in the section about Ham and his father's nakedness, the preacher comments on other phrases and words from the passage, such as "nakedness," "told," and "cursed by Canaan."

Note how these illustrations from Scripture adorn and add to the biblical text. The terrible punishments visited upon Ham apparently develop out of the "curse" pronounced by Noah. The story of Noah's drunkenness is an imaginative application to life of the words of the text that Noah "became drunk." Of course, the story reflects Jewish disgust for the unclean pig.

Now that we have examined the *formal characteristics* of the sermon, let us explore the *message* it conveyed.

The main thrust of the sermon is a warning to the audience against too close an association with or dependence upon the soil. However, this warning is given against the background of a view of reality in which the world is divided into sacred and profane, holy and common. In this view of reality the soil was associated with the secular and the profane. In a society which prized the study of Torah and ritual purity because they were associated with God, common and profane things were distant from God, to be tolerated, but not to be the main object of one's striving.

After the text is stated and Noah is identified with the profane, Cain and Uzziah are also cited as negative examples. Everyone would know that Cain was "a tiller of the ground" (Gen 4:2) and that God rejected his "offering of the fruit of the ground" (Gen 4:3) in favor of Abel's sheep. Hence, Cain became the first murderer. Thus Cain, a thoroughly despicable character in Jewish tradition, is treated only briefly.

Noah is more complex. The Bible specifically says that "Noah was a righteous man" and that he "walked with God." (Gen 6:9) Accordingly, God saved him from the flood. However, after leaving the ark, he planted a vineyard and turned his attention to the soil. All kinds of trouble thereby came upon Noah and his sons.

The preacher continues to explore the passage and tells the punishments that were visited upon Ham for looking at the nakedness of his father.

The reader becomes aware that the simple thrust of the sermon is set within a larger theological framework when the preacher turns to the evil inclination which accounts for the multiplication of sin in this life. While the check upon the evil inclination is the study and practice of God's will, that is, Torah, the battle against the evil inclination is finally won only in the world to come in the resurrection. Note how realistically the rabbis conceived the resurrected self to be. Since the human body was thought to consist of 248 parts, so the resurrected self would be whole, even the slave's eye and tooth being restored.

The third negative example is Uzziah who "loved the soil." His act of self-assertion in attempting to approach the Holy God as a priest, although in reality he was a layman and profane because of the soil, is punished with leprosy.

Finally, the main thrust of the sermon is summarized beautifully in the last line: "he neglected Torah and offered himself to the soil." In addition to the last line of the sermon, there are two specific passages where the preacher makes a direct application to the audience. Both these applications are made by means of a common rule which the rabbis used to interpret Scripture and to clarify legal discussions. The name of the rule is best translated "light and heavy" because it designates an inference from the less important to the more important and vice versa. The first instance is found at the end of the story of Noah's drunkenness in the following sentence: "What? (Did all this happen to) Noah the righteous one whose praise the Holy One Blessed Be He proclaimed? What then of the rest of humanity? *How much the more!*" "How much the more" indicates an application from the heavy to the light, that is, from Noah to the rest of humanity. If Noah can fall to such a state, what about the rest of you in this congregation? So avoid drunkenness.

The second application, in this case from light to heavy, is applied to the law about slavery in Exod 21:26 which is quoted in the sermon. The preacher specifically asks whether it is not a matter of light to heavy. If, under certain conditions, slaves go from slavery to freedom in this life, then, is it not appropriate that God's people, enslaved by the evil inclination in this life, should go to the greater freedom from sin in the life to come, in which, in addition, their bodies will be restored and made whole? Such a note of hope was usually found in a sermon at the end of the pattern in the Tanchuma. Such a note is particularly appropriate for this sermon which conveys such a gloomy picture of the human condition.

Another technical point needs clarification. A well-known rabbinic theological principle is exemplified in the punishments visited upon Ham. Ham received "measure for measure." Ham's misdeeds were rewarded with exact retribution: every deed, whether good or bad finds its exact compensation.[5]

---

[5] E. Urbach, *The Sages: Their Concepts and Beliefs* (Jerusalem: Magnes Press, 1975), 438–439.

IV. The Synagogue Homily and the New Testament

A. Formal Characteristics

The homily we have just read is a fine example of literary art and should be appreciated for that reason alone. Nevertheless, the following pages intend to show the relationship between the form of the sermon from the Tanchuma and that of a sermon found in the Gospel of John.

In his pioneering work entitled *Bread From Heaven*, Peder Borgen has described the characteristics of a sermon in John 6:31–58.

The sermon begins with a statement of several words from Exod 16:4 supplemented by the words "gave" and "eat," apparently quoted from Exod 16:15.

> Our fathers ate the manna in the wilderness; as it is written, 'He gave them bread from heaven to eat.' (John 6:31)

The sermon ends with these words:

> This is the bread which came down from heaven, not such as the fathers ate and died; he who eats this bread will live forever. (John 6:58)

Note the following formal characteristics. Key words from the text cited at the beginning of the sermon are repeated at the end in order to form an inclusion. Also, the conclusion: "he who eats this bread will live forever," sums up the main thrust of the whole sermon.

Words from the text, such as "gave," "bread," "from heaven," and "eat" are commented on and paraphrased throughout the sermon. These words are systematically discussed. Another characteristic of the sermon is the introduction of a subordinate OT text from Isa 54:13 in John 6:45. Borgen summarized the three main characteristics of the pattern in the following words:

> 1) There is a correspondence between the opening and closing parts of the homily. At the same time the closing statement sums up points from the homily. . . .
> 2) In addition to the main quotation from the OT, the text, there is at least one subordinate quotation, also from the OT.
> 3) Words from the text are paraphrased or quoted in the homily.[6]

In addition to the three main characteristics of the homily, Borgen also notes that the homily reflects a whole passage or pericope rather than a single verse from the OT.

---

[6] P. Borgen, *Bread From Heaven* (Leiden: Brill, 1965), 47.

There are striking similarities between the pattern discovered by Borgen and the formal features of the sermon from the Tanchuma (see above). Both sermons open with a text and a word/words from the text are quoted and explained throughout the sermons. Both sermons end with a reference back to the opening text and both conclusions summarize the main thrust of the message. Also, both homilies reflect a whole passage, not just the opening text.

On the other hand there are some differences. Not all the formal features of the Tanchuma sermon are found in the Johannine sermon. Nevertheless, total congruence is not to be expected in a form that is not so rigidly fixed as that of the proem. Also, within two of the same formal features there are slight differences between the two sermons. While the Tanchuma comments on just one word from the initial text, the Johannine sermon comments on at least four. Only one subordinate text is cited in John while the Tanchuma cites a large number. However, in studying sermons from Philo that exemplify the same pattern, Borgen noted that more than one subordinate text could be cited, thereby establishing the existence of variations within the formal feature.

What does it mean that essentially the same homiletical pattern is found both in the NT (and in Philo) and in a much later literary sermon from the Tanchuma? Perhaps the similarities in form are just coincidental. Could later Palestinian rabbis who wrote in Hebrew have borrowed a homiletical pattern from the Greek New Testament or the Greek works of Philo? Later rabbis would hardly copy a pattern from a rejected book like the NT, although they may have known Philo. Rather, the more realistic explanation is that the first-century sermons of John, Paul, and Philo—and the later rabbinic sermons—all made use of a traditional Jewish pattern which Jewish preachers used for hundreds of years. All three first-century writers were strongly influenced by Jewish religious thought, one element of which was a homiletical pattern used in the synagogues. This homiletical pattern apparently possessed great vitality, for it commanded the respect of preachers for several hundred years![7]

The isolation of a homiletical pattern common to the NT, Philo, and later rabbinic sermons is a positive result of this investigation. However, the attempts of several interpreters to find proem homilies in the NT must be evaluated negatively. Attempts to force this form upon NT passages have not succeeded and have not met with approval.[8] As we

---

[7] G. Vermes, *Jesus and the World of Judaism* (Philadelphia: Fortress Press, 1984), chap. 6, esp. p. 85. While Vermes does not discuss homiletical patterns, he makes a strong case that "the NT and the rabbinic doctrine both derive from a common source, viz., Jewish traditional teaching." I am suggesting that one aspect of "Jewish traditional teaching" was a first-century homiletical pattern.

[8] See Heinemann's critique of two such recent attempts ("The Proem in the Aggadic Midrashim: A Form-Critical Study," p. 104, n. 14a and p. 121, n. 78).

have seen, the proem form probably was not used until after A.D. 70: this "upside-down" form was designed to introduce the reading from the Torah and apparently flourished only between A.D. 200 and A.D. 500. While the earliest Jewish-Christian preachers adopted the sermon from the synagogue service they knew, the sermon took the form of a comment on the biblical lesson. Hence, to read the proem form back into the NT is an anachronism.

Indeed, the primary error in Peder Borgen's research has been his identification of the homiletical pattern he discovered with the proem found in later Palestinean homilies. Unfortunately, the editors or copyists of the collections of homilies often inserted the first verse of the passage to which the proem leads as a conclusion, also at the beginning of the proem before the "remote" text as a kind of chapter heading. Since, therefore, the first verse of the Pentateuchal passage appeared at both the beginning and the end, Borgen, as well as other scholars, was misled in making the identification with the proem.

B. A Common View of Reality

In addition to sharing the formal characteristics of a common homiletical pattern, how do texts of this type help us to understand aspects of early Christian literature better?

The NT writers and the preachers and compilers of rabbinic homilies had much in common in that they shared a common way of looking at reality. In looking at much of the NT from the perspective of these later Jewish sermons, we see it, so to speak, from the backside. Especially, with respect to the Gospels, we see much of it set within its native environment. A number of examples will suffice.

Perhaps the most striking example is the fact that they share some of the same rules for interpreting Scripture and applying religious truth to life. Specifically, both the Tanchuma sermon and Jesus use the same inference from light to heavy. The rabbinic preacher twice used this rule to apply a passage in the sermon to the audience. Jesus also used this rule to urge his audience to pray. In Matt 7:9 Jesus tells this story from everyday life: "Or what man of you, if his sons ask him for a loaf, will give him a stone?" Then in verse 11 he moves from the light to the heavy in exhorting the audience to pray. First the light—"If you then, who are evil, know how to give good gifts to your children,"—then the heavy—"how much more (Note the same phrase) will your Father who is in heaven give good things to those who ask him?" Thus if God is so willing to give good gifts, you ought to ask in prayer.

Indeed, this very common rule of interpretation mirrors a way of thinking about reality and God in both the NT and the rabbinic homilies. In both literatures this same rule is the key that unlocks the meaning of parables. For example, in the parable of the Lost Coin (Luke 15:8–10) interpretation begins with the "light" or story from everyday life, and moves to the "heavy" or God's relationship with people. The story from everyday life is summarized in this line: "Rejoice with me, for I have found the coin which I had lost." (15:9b) God's relationship with people is given in 15:10: "Even so, I tell you, there is joy before the angels of God over one sinner who repents." Like the rabbis, Jesus wanted to reverence the Name and so employed the circumlocution "joy before the angels of God." However, the sentence simply means that God rejoices. Hence the parable means: as the woman rejoices over finding the lost coin, so God rejoices over finding the lost sinner. Thought moves from earth to heaven and from light to heavy. God is the supreme reality—the heavy—while we are created and derivative—the light.

Both the Jewish homily and portions of the NT "live" out of the Hebrew Bible. In addition to the fact that the homily began and ended with quotes from the OT, every point in the homily had to be "proved" from the OT. Much the same is true of certain writers of the NT whose passages are replete with quotations from the OT. Many of these quotes are introduced by formulas. While the NT citation formulas are rarely as stylized as Rabbi Oshaya's citation formula, the formulas do bear witness to the authority of the Hebrew Bible for NT writers.

Rabbi Oshaya's proem offers additional examples of significant points of contact between the thought-world of the NT and the rabbinic homilies. The main thrust of the sermon is the striking assertion that Torah existed before the world (universe) was created and was actually the pattern or blueprint according to which God created the world. Similarly, several NT writers attribute pre-existence to Christ and the Gospel of John even asserts that "all things were made through Him" (1:3). Could the NT writers have been influenced by Jewish speculation about the pre-existence of Wisdom/Torah as they attributed pre-existence to the resurrected Lord? Leading NT scholars believe so![9]

Reverence for the Divine Name is another indication of a common thought-world. Rabbi Oshaya avoids mention of the term "God" altogether by using the circumlocution "The Holy One, Blessed Be He." In the parable of the Lost Sheep, Jesus speaks of *"joy in heaven* over one sinner who repents" (Luke 15:7) in order to avoid saying that God rejoices. Frequently, the passive voice is used to avoid using the term "God." Nevertheless, the reverence for God's name that we find in the NT is carried to its completion in Oshaya's sermon where the term "God" is not used at all.

A few other examples should be mentioned. In the story of Noah's drunkenness, Satan is introduced quite naturally and becomes a partici-

---

[9] R. Brown, *The Gospel According to John*, 29 (Anchor Bible; New York: Doubleday, 1966), esp. 520–524.

pant in the action. Similarly, in the NT, Satan plays a significant role. He is the "strong man" (Mark 3:27) whom Jesus binds before performing the exorcisms that so characterize his ministry. Indeed, at the beginning of Jesus' ministry, Satan tests Jesus in the wilderness (Matt 4:1–11 and Luke 4:1–13). Also, at the close of the ministry, "Satan entered into Judas called Iscariot" (Luke 22:3) before Judas betrayed Jesus.

We read that Ham was punished "measure for measure." There is an echo of this teaching in Matt 7:2 in the statement: "the measure you give will be the measure you get." Here, however, the statement is intended to reinforce the teaching: "Judge not, that you be not judged" (Matt 7:1).

In the Tanchuma the preacher was concerned about ritual purity and the division between sacred and profane. The Pharisees, who meet us in the pages of the gospels, felt this same concern. Indeed, this is why Jesus teaches the parable of the Lost Coin (see Luke 15:1–2) to the Pharisees.

Of greater significance for NT studies than the presence of a Jewish homiletical pattern is the light these homilies shed on the thought-world out of which the NT emerged. They call attention to the Jewish roots and background of the NT and illumine many of its obscurities.

V. Annotated Bibliography

A comprehensive study of a homiletical pattern in the NT is found in P. Borgen, *Bread From Heaven* (Leiden: Brill, 1965). L. Ginzberg, *The Legends of the Jews* (Philadelphia: Jewish Publication Society, 1913) has compiled a monumental selection of stories drawn from varied sources. Excerpts from the sermon from the Tanchuma are found in vol. 1, 167–169 and the footnotes are located in vol. 5, 190. The best single work on the proem is J. Heinemann, "The Proem in the Aggadic Midrashim: A Form-Critical Study," *Studies in Aggadah and Folk-Literature: Scripta Hierosolymitana XXII* (Jerusalem, 1971a), 100–200. Also, his article on "Preaching. In the Talmudic Period," *Encyclopedia Judaica*, vol. 13 (Jerusalem, 1971b), 994–998, is a model of lucidity and brevity. Not mentioned in the foregoing chapter, but related to any discussion of the Jewish or NT homilies is the possible existence of a triennial lectionary. Again, J. Heinemann gives the definitive research in "The Triennial Lectionary Cycle," *Journal of Jewish Studies*, 1968, 41–48. In the foregoing discussion the technical term *Midrash* has been avoided. However, the Jewish homily is set within its midrashic context and a good explanation of the term is given by M.P. Miller, "Midrash," *Intrepreter's Dictionary of the Bible, Supplementary Volume*, 593–597. A widely used reference work is H.L. Strack, *Introduction to the Talmud and Midrash* (New York, 1959). His brief description of the Tanchuma is given on p. 212 and of Midrash Rabbah: Genesis, on pp. 217–18.

CHAPTER 4
THE DIATRIBE

Stanley K. Stowers
Brown University

I. Introduction

The history of research on the diatribe falls quite naturally into three periods. First is the period from 1880 to 1910 in which intensive work on the diatribe led to a consensus about its history and characteristics. Second, the period from 1910 to the Second World War was a time when scholars criticized and evaluated the earlier consensus. Little new basic research was carried out in this period. Third, since the Second World War, scholars have gained a renewed appreciation for the earlier research while carefully weighing the criticisms of the second period.

This characterization of research on the diatribe does not apply to New Testament studies, only to classical scholarship. Before the First World War many New Testament scholars were knowledgeable in classical philology and worked in concert with classical scholars on the diatribe. In 1910, Rudolf Bultmann published his famous dissertation on Paul and the diatribe. Bultmann's work gathered the results of the earlier consensus and applied them to Paul. The year after his book appeared, two scholars launched major attacks on the earlier consensus which have been widely influential in classical scholarship. New Testament scholars, however, have depended almost entirely on Bultmann's work, increasingly isolating themselves from classical scholarship, and created a world of theological and "history of religions" caricature which is unrecognizable to the classical scholar. Only recently has there been a renewed interest in relating current classical scholarship to early Christianity and thus renewed work among some New Testament scholars on the diatribe.

In 1881 U. von Wilamowitz-Moellendorf wrote an essay, "Teles, the Cynic Preacher."[1] This essay set the pattern for later understanding of

[1] In *Antigonos von Karystos* (Philologische Untersuchungen 4; Berlin: Weidmanische Buchandlung, 1881).

the diatribe. Wilamowitz emphasized that the fragments of this third century B.C. Cynic teacher, belonged to the genre of "preaching." It was the genre of the itinerant philosophical preacher which put philosophy in a form for the common man on the street corner and in the marketplace. Wilamowitz described the diatribe as a kind of half-dialogue which resulted from a mixing of philosophical dialogue with rhetorical declamation. Otto Hense tried to show that Teles had largely copied the eclectic sophist, Bion of Borysthenes.[2] It became widely held that Bion was the originator of the diatribe and numerous works tried to prove that later writings with diatribe-like style had used Bion. Scholars looked for common characteristics of diatribe-style in numerous ancient authors. This resulted in a very broad consensus that the works of several authors were either diatribes or contained the style of the diatribe: Teles-Bion, Musonius Rufus, Philo, Epictetus, Plutarch, Dio of Prusa, Maximus of Tyre and Seneca. Other authors were also sometimes included but with much less agreement. Due to the prominence of Stoics in the list and the supposed origin of the diatribe with the cynicizing Bion, the standard designation for the "genre" became the "Cynic-Stoic diatribe."

Paul Wendland provided a synthesis for the earlier work on the diatribe when he proposed a history of its development to explain the diversity and commonality in the canon of authors. The genre as developed first by Bion was witty, lively and entertaining. Bion mixed seriousness with humor and often used vulgarity. In contrast, the moral treatises and speeches of later authors like Musonius, Plutarch and Dio were wholly serious and often far from lively. Wendland said that the earlier lively diatribe of Bion had evolved, as post classical philosophy became more pedantic, into the later diatribe. Wendland explained the anomaly of Epictetus' lively diatribes in the later period as somehow a throwback to the earlier style.

In the decades just before and just after the turn of the century, C. F. Georg Heinrici was already using the diatribe to shed light on the letters of Paul.[3] Rudolf Bultmann's dissertation, *Der Stil der Paulinischen Predigt und die kynisch-stoische Diatribe*, owes much to three scholars. Bultmann was stimulated by Wendland's study of Philo which showed how a Jew could make use of motifs and stylistic elements from the diatribe. Henricus Weber's *De Senecae philosophi dicendi genere Bioneo*[4] provided Bultmann with a detailed stylistic analysis of the diatribe and categories to use in the analysis of Paul's letters. Bultmann's teacher, Johnannes Weiss had studied Paul's rhetoric, demonstrating the applicability of ancient Greek rhetoric to his letters.

[2] *Teletis reliquiae* (Tübingen: Teubner, 1889) 2nd ed., 1909.
[3] See especially, *Der litterarische Charakter der neutestamentlischen Schriften* (Leipzig: Durr, 1908).
[4] (Marburg: F. Sommering, 1895).

Bultmann showed that Paul's letters, especially Romans, shared stylistic traits with the diatribe. He assumed along with the older consensus that the diatribe was a form of popular philosophical preaching to the masses. Thus he concluded that the diatribe-style of the letters reflected Paul's style and method of oral preaching. Nevertheless, Butlmann insisted that Paul's use of the style was superficial because the apostle's thought was shaped by faith rather than reason.

The year after Bultmann's book appeared, Adolph Bonhöffer and Otto Halbauer launched attacks on the older consensus which opened the way for a major reassessment of the diatribe.[5] Most importantly, Halbauer showed that *diatribē* was never used for a clearly defined literary genre. Rather the term was used primarily for the teaching activity—e.g. conversations and lectures—in ancient schools and secondarily for records and literary imitations of such teaching discourse. Many scholars have sharply attacked the belief that Bion founded the supposed genre and there is no evidence that Bion's discourses actually follow the style of other authors who were suppose to have imitated him in their diatribes. Above all, it is an unfortunate misuse to equate diatribe with "popular-philosophical" literature in general. Frequently, writers have done this, describing works belonging to dozens of poetic and non-poetic genres and subgenres as diatribes. This only obscures and confuses the issues of definition. "Diatribe" can only be a useful concept if we use it in a way which approximates ancient useage: A term for teaching activity in the schools, literary imitations of that activity, or for writings which employ the rhetorical and pedagogical style typical of diatribes in the schools.

Recent scholarship has reconsidered Bultmann's work in light of criticism of the older consensus. Paul's use of the style does not imply that he was a Cynic-like street preacher since the diatribe does not represent that sort of polemical harangue. Instead, the style evokes the student-teacher relationship and the situation of the philosophical school. Bultmann accepted Wendland's history and characterization of the diatribe. Wendland's division of the diatribe into a lively entertaining hellenistic type and a later didactic type has been discredited. The differences in style among authors is not to be explained by historical evolution of a literary genre created by Bion but by the varied adaptations of the school style, by different authors, in varied historical and rhetorical circumstances. There is, in fact, no evidence that Bion employed the dialogical style of the diatribe. Epictetus' lively style is hardly a throwback to Bion. There is evidence that Musonius' original diatribes, as opposed to Lucius' paraphrases and summaries, were as lively and

---

[5] *Epiktet und des Neue Testament* (RGVV 10; Giessen: Töpelmann, 1911); for Halbauer, see bibliography.

dialogical as Epictetus' diatribes. Thus, one ought to think in terms of adaptation of a style rather than the decline of a literary genre.

II. Formal Features of Diatribes

Since the style of the diatribe is derived from the pedagogical activity of the philosophical school, the diatribe's characteristic formal features can be best understood in light of that activity. Aulus Gellius (*Attic Nights* 1.26) provides a brief account of what happened in the school of the philosopher Taurus.

> During the course of a diatribe *(in diatriba)*, I once asked Taurus if a wise man got angry. For after his daily readings he often allowed [the students] to ask whatever questions they wished. On this occasion he discussed the sickness or passion of anger seriously and for a long time, setting forth both what the books of the ancients and his own commentaries had to say. Then he turned to me who had asked the question and said, "This is what I think about getting angry . . . but also hear what Plutarch says. . . ."[6]

One hears about four major forms of pedagogical activity in philosophical schools. First, teachers gave lectures which ranged from formal discourses that were read, to very informal sermon-like exhortations. The "reading" *(lectio)* mentioned by Gellius may have been a lecture. The answer Taurus gave to Gellius' question would also qualify as a sort of impromptu lecture, including the discussion of older philosophical authorities, Taurus' own views, and a long anecdote about Taurus' teacher, Plutarch. Second, the exegesis and discussion of texts was important.[7] Some of Epictetus' diatribes spring from ethical questions raised during the exegesis of texts which preceeded the diatribes recorded by Arrian. The "readings" of Taurus may be his discussion of texts. Third, our sources frequently describe general class discussions, sometimes in the form of questions and answers. Fourth, the teacher often picked out one particular student and carried on a dialogue in front of the class.

Such classroom activity could be recorded and published or the lecture-question and answer-dialogical pedagogy of the school could be adapted as a literary style for written works. Arrian composed the diatribes of Epictetus from notes probably taken in shorthand. Another student, Lucius, wrote the diatribes of his teacher, Musonius Rufus, but

---

[6] The translation is my own.

[7] The study of texts in the philosophical schools deserves more attention from scholars. See the following comments: Adolf Bonhöffer, *Die Ethik des Stoikers Epictet* (Stuttgart: Ferdinand Enke, 1894) 2; Ivo Bruns, *De schola Epicteti* (Kiel, 1897) 2–4; *Epictète Entretiens*, ed. and transl. Joseph Souilhe (Collection des Universites de France; Paris: Societe D'Édition "Les Belles Lettres", 1975) 1.XXXIII–XXXV.

with more summarizing and less verbatum quotation than Arrian. Diatribes could also be pure literary fictions which simulated the dialogue and lecture of the schools. Aristippus, a follower of Socrates, is said to have "written six books of diatribes" (*Diogenes Laertius* 2.84). In Plutarch's, *The Face which Appears in the Orb of the Moon*, Lamprias recounts a discussion in which he took part. That narrative contains an account of a yet earlier discussion: "Our friend in his diatribe won approval by this proposition . . ." (929B). Plutarch has used the form of narrating elaborate fictitious diatribes, i.e. scholastic discussions, in order to present his own ideas. The characteristic form of extant diatribes from Teles in the third century B.C. onward is that of a lecture or written treatise which discusses common moral-philosophical topics enlivened at various points by fictitious dialogue and questions from imaginary auditors. Diatribes which record actual school activity contain discussions both with real and imaginary discussion partners.

There is no typical structure to a diatribe. It is not a dialogue in the literary tradition of Plato and Xenophon, although diatribes frequently contain dialogues and the conversational style of the classroom. The larger form of the work is a lecture or treatise on a particular moral or philosophical topic, e.g., divine providence, self-sufficiency, contentment, freedom, self-control, anger, old age, pleasure.

The diatribal authors simulate direct address in their discourses by creating an imaginary discussion partner, and by means of direct address to their audiences. The dialogical element in the diatribe takes several forms and within limits varies considerably from author to author. One method consists of short exchanges of questions and answers. Often this is in the Socratic manner with the teacher leading the fictitious interlocutor by means of pointed questions, frequently posing absurdities which the interlocutor must strongly reject. This method is prominent in Teles, Epictetus and Dio Chrysostom. Sometimes the interlocutor asks the questions and the teacher answers. A technique of many authors is to string a series of objections and false conclusions from the interlocutor throughout the lecture or treatise. The interlocutor's question draws a false inference from which the author wishes to guard himself or poses a typical objection to the author's line of reasoning. The teacher's answer, then, serves as a transition to a new topic or step in the argumentation. A series of such objections may become a structuring principle for a discourse. Objections and false conclusions are often rejected with strong negatives or an oath-formula, e.g. *mē genoito* (By no means!).

Diatribes also effect their style of direct address by means of brief speeches where the teacher turns from his real audience to address an imaginary individual. Typically but not always, these are sharp censorious words which rebuke the interlocutor for some vice or pattern of behavior. These apostrophes tend to function as characterizations of the interlocutor. Addresses to an interlocutor employ vice lists, rhetorical questions, vocatives such as "O man", "fool" and "sir". They are usually spoken in the second person singular. The writer or speaker tends to maintain contact at various points with the audience in a way which is similar to letter-writing style. Diatribal and epistolary styles combine easily. The author may turn from the interlocutor or general argumentative discourse to exhort the audience or address a question to it.

Other elements of style vary widely according to the cultural-educational backgrounds, philosophical stances and immediate purposes of the particular authors. Nevertheless, there are a number of rhetorical features which characteristically serve the didactic and hortatory purposes of the diatribe. The style tends to be conversational with parataxis and elliptical expressions, although some authors use periods. Short sentences with simple conversational syntax predominate in dialogical sections. Rhetorical figures such as isocola, parallelism and antithesis are popular. Rhetorical questions, often in a series, are very common. The style is certainly didactic and often hortatory. Thus, much use is made of quotations from poets and philosophers in the form of maxims and brief citations. Anecdotes or chreiai, comparisons and especially examples from history and legend are very important. Irony and sarcasm is prominent. Virtue and vice lists illustrate conceptions of the good and evil person. Some authors like to personify abstract ideas such as death, poverty and wealth.

III. The Text:
Epictetus, *Concerning Anxiety* (*Discourses* 2.13)

Epictetus' discourse on anxiety is an example of a diatribe in an actual school setting. Epictetus was born in Hierapolis of Phrygia in about A.D. 50 and died about 125. He became the slave of Nero's freedman, Epaphroditus, who allowed him to attend the school of the Stoic philosopher, Musonius Rufus. Epictetus first taught in Rome and then established a Stoic school in Nicopolis which attracted many students who became distinguished figures.

Epictetus' diatribe on anxiety was delivered to his students in Nicopolis and recorded in shorthand by one of them, Arrian. Philosophy for Epictetus is not primarily a theoretical discipline but a way of life. The purpose of this diatribe is hortatory. Epictetus tries to turn his students from false beliefs and practices which cause anxiety. Through the censure of what is false and the encouragement of what is good and true in his students, he hopes to build character which is in harmony with Reason or God.

Epictetus' style, syntax, and in certain areas, his vocabulary, are so similar to Paul's that scholars have engaged in a major debate over whether Paul used Epictetus, or Epictetus used Paul. Rather than actual dependence, however, a better explanation comes from recognizing that both had extensive experience as teachers in the Hellenistic world and that both shared a widely influential "school style", the style of the diatribe.

Concerning Anxiety

When I see a person who is anxious, I say to myself, "What is it that he wants?" For if he did not want something that was outside of his control, how could he be anxious? Thus, the cithara player is not anxious when singing alone, but when he enters the theatre, even if he sings beautifully and plays the cithara well. For he wants not only to sing well, but also to be admired, and that is no longer under his control. Thus he displays confidence where he possesses skill. Bring any lay man before him that you will, and the cithra player will pay no attention. But in an area where he is ignorant and untrained, there he is anxious. What is the significance of this? He does not know what a crowd is or the meaning of its praise. Certainly he has learned to pluck the highest and lowest strings, but what the praise of the crowd is, and its function in life, that he neither knows nor has studied. Thus he must necessarily tremble and turn pale.[a]

Therefore, when I see someone who is afraid, I cannot say that he is not a cithara player, but I can say something else about him, and not just one thing but several. First of all, I call him a stranger and I say: "This man does not know where on earth he is, but though being an inhabitant for a long time, he is ignorant of the city's laws, and customs, and what is and is not permitted. And he has never entertained a lawyer to speak to him and explain the laws. Yet he does not write a will unless he knows how it should be done or else he gets an expert—but without a lawyer he exercises desire and aversion and choice and design and purpose. What do I mean by, "without a lawyer"? He does not know that he wants things not given to him, and wants to avoid the inevitable, and he does not know either what belongs to him or to another. But if he did know, he would never feel obstructed, nor hindered, nor anxious.[b]

---

[a] The diatribe begins with the concrete example of the cithara player in order to illustrate the source of anxiety. Such illustrations and comparisons are common in the diatribal literature. Epictetus presents the illustration in the form of a conversation with himself. Often the "I" in such self-conversations is purely rhetorical (see Rom 7:7–25). The diatribes of Epictetus and other authors more frequently begin with a rather theoretical discussion of a thesis or topic in the third person.

[b] From his initial example, Epictetus deduces some general observations about the "anxious person". This will allow him to introduce an imaginary interlocutor who characterizes the "anxious person" in the dialogues which follow. In the second paragraph he says that the anxious

[*Imaginary Dialogue Follows*]
—For how could he? Does one fear what is not evil?[c]
—No!
—What then? Does he fear what is truly evil, but in his own power to prevent?
—By no means![d]
—If then, the things that are not a matter of moral choice are neither good nor evil, but all matters of moral choice are under our control, and no one can take them away from us, or procure them for us against our will, where is there any place for anxiety? But we are anxious about our little bodies, our few possessions, about what Caesar will think, yet are not anxious about that which is within us. We are not anxious to keep from conceiving a false idea, are we?
—No! For that is under my control.
—What about making a choice contrary to nature?
—No, not about that.

Therefore when you [sing.][e] see someone who is pale, just as the physician judging from his color says, "his spleen is affected, and his liver is affected," so also you [sing.] say, "his desire and aversion are affected; he is not doing well; he has a fever."[f] For nothing else changes a person's color, or makes him tremble, or his teeth chatter: "Keep shifting knees and resting on one foot and then another" (Homer, *Illiad* 13. 281).[g]

Thus Zeno was not anxious before he met Antigonus. For Antigonus

person is one who is ignorant of human character, having never entertained an expert, i.e., a philosopher. Thus he worries about things that are not under his control and takes no care for what is. Note that Epictetus continues the same style of self-conversation as in the first paragraph.

[c] Epictetus conducts the dialogue which follows in the "Socratic" manner. He asks pointed questions to which the interlocutor must logically answer as Epictetus intends. These questions are meant to point out and dispel the interlocutor's erroneous beliefs and attitudes and to lead him to see the truth.

[d] The first two sets of questions and replies take a characteristic diatribal form: A short interjective question, i.e., "For how could he?" (*pōs gar ou*), "What then?" (*ti de*); short questions which obviously require negative answers; a short and sharp rejection of the question by the interlocutor, i.e., "no" (*ou*); "By no means" (*oudamōs*). Compare Rom 3:3–9.

[e] It is very important to realize that Epictetus continues to speak to the interlocutor using the second person singular even though the question and answer dialogue has ended. Much confusion in the exegesis of Paul's letters, especially Romans, could be avoided if exegetes would take note of Paul's addressing of fictitious interlocutors: see, for instance, Rom 2:1–16; 2:17–29.

[f] Epictetus compares anxiety resulting from failure to recognize what is and is not under one's control, to physical illness. The metaphor of moral character flaws as illness and the likening of the philosopher to a doctor are extremely common in the diatribe. See Abraham J. Malherbe, "Medical Imagery in the Pastoral Epistles", *Texts and Testaments* ed. E. March (San Antonio: Trinity University, 1980) 19–35.

[g] Quotations from the poets, especially Homer, the tragedians and comics, are very frequent in the diatribal literature. They add authority to the argument but tend to have an illustrative function.

did not have power over anything Zeno valued, and that over which Antigonus did have power, Zeno did not care about. But Antigonus was anxious before he met Zeno, and reasonably so. For he wanted to please him and that was outside of his control. But Zeno did not desire to please him, just as an artist does not care about pleasing someone who is ignorant of art.[h]

Do I want to please you [sing.]?[i] For what reason? Do you know the standards by which one man judges another? Have you made it a concern to know what a good person is, what an evil person, and how each becomes that way? Why then are you yourself not a good person?

[*Imaginary Dialogue Follows*]

—How, he says,[j] do you know that I am not a good person?[k]

—Because no good person grieves or groans, no good person cries, no good person turns pale, trembles, and says, "How will he receive me? How will he listen to me?" You slave! As it seems best to *him*.[l] Why, then, are you concerned about that which belongs to another? Then is it not his mistake if he receives badly what you have to say?

—Yes, of course.

—Is it possible for one person to make the mistake and another to be morally harmed by it?

—No!

—Why, then, are you anxious over what is the concern of another?

—Yes, but I am anxious about how I shall speak to him.[m]

—So then, are you not allowed to speak to him as you will?

---

[h] This paragraph is a common form of an *exemplum*, a moral model and example from history or legend. Here it is in the form of the contrasting positive and negative examples of Zeno and Antigonus, respectively. The story was well known so that Epictetus only has to show how it applies to his point about anxiety. Zeno was the founder of the Stoic school of philosophy and Antigonus was a Greek King.

[i] In what follows, Epictetus again provokes a dialogue with the fictitious interlocutor. The tone now changes. Epictetus addresses the interlocutor in a personally sharp and censorious way. The interlocutor's character as the anxious person, or more precisely, the anxious and therefore inconsistent and pretentious student of philosophy, begins to emerge.

[j] Note that the words of the interlocutor are not usually introduced by "he says" or the like. This sentence is an exception. Among the representative authors the way the interlocutor's words are introduced varies considerably.

[k] For the sake of clarity, my translation often fills out elliptical expressions and the extremely terse language of every day conversation. This sentence would be literally translated as "How, he says, am I not?"

[l] This passage of censorious address to the interlocutor shows characteristic features of such texts: indicting rhetorical questions which characterize the interlocutor's vice; a harsh term of address e.g., slave, wretch, fool. Compare Rom 2:1–5; 17–24; I Cor 15:36.

[m] Here the interlocutor voices a characteristic objection to what Epictetus is saying. It echoes objections already made above. Such objections are introduced in many different ways but often begin with the adversative *"alla."* Objections often suddenly appear in non-dialogical texts. Compare Rom 4:1–2; 9:19; 11:19; I Cor 6:12, 13, 18; 15:35.

—But I fear that I will be rejected.
—You are not afraid of being rejected when you write the name Dio are you?
—By no means!
—For what reason? Is it not because you have practiced writing?
—Yes, of course.
—What then? If you were about to read, wouldn't you also feel confident?
—Yes, the same.
—For what reason? Because every art has a certain strength and confidence which belongs to that skill. Have you, then, not practiced speaking? And what else did you practice in school?
—Syllogisms and arguments with equivocal premises.
—For what purpose? Was it not so that you might be skillful in argument? And does not "skillfully" mean timely, steadfastly, intelligently, and even without mistakes and embarrassment, and on top of all this, with confidence?
—Yes!
—If you are on a horse and have ridden on to a plain against a footsoldier, are you anxious if you are well trained and the other is not?
—Yes, but he has the power to kill me.

Then tell the truth, wretch, and do not boast, or claim to be a philosopher, or do not be ignorant of your masters![n] But as long as they have this hold on you through your body, follow everyone who is stronger than you. But Socrates practiced speaking—Socrates who conversed as he did with the tyrants, the judges, and in prison. Diogenes had practiced speaking—Diogenes who spoke with Alexander as he did, to Philip, to the pirates, to the man who bought him—But as for you, amble off to your own affairs and never again leave them, go into your corner and sit down, and spin syllogisms and offer them to others

"In you the city has found no leader."[o]

IV. The Diatribe and Early Christian Literature

The letters of Paul are the earliest pieces of Christian literature to show the influence of the diatribe. Some have suggested that Paul

---

[n] The diatribe concludes with a strongly censorious apostrophe to the interlocutor. The boasting and inconsistency of would-be philosophers and students of philosophy is an important motif in the diatribe. Compare Rom 2:17–29. Such apostrophes are certainly important in the diatribe but Epictetus' use of one as a conclusion is unusual. The real targets of the censure are, of course, students in Epictetus' classroom who might have the traits which Epictetus criticizes in the interlocutor. The function of such apostrophes is hortatory.

[o] The author of this concluding verse is unknown.

acquired the style through "Hellenistic Judaism" and the sermon of the Hellenistic Synagogue. We have no evidence for the latter but any artisan and traveller of the cities in the Greek East could be expected to know of the diatribe. Schools often operated in public view, a teacher gathering a circle of students in a market, gymnasium, or stoa. There are descriptions of passers-by stopping to listen to a philosopher lecturing to his disciples in a public place. Satirists, comic playwrights and moralists parodied the philosophers' teaching style assuming that their audiences were familiar with it. Paul himself was both a teacher and man of the Hellenistic world. Understanding the style of the diatribe gives us insight into Paul's missionary purposes and practices.

As any other writer, Paul's employment of diatribal techniques is an adaptation to his own purposes and rhetorical style. The dialogical style of the diatribe is most prominent in Romans. He uses it to present himself as a teacher to a church where he wants to preach his own particular gospel concerning the redemption of the Gentiles. In 2:17–29 Paul introduces and characterizes a Jewish interlocutor whom he censures for failing to be a light to the Gentiles. Diatribal dialogues with this interlocutor ensue in 3:1–9 and 3:27–4:2 where Paul urges hm to give up his boastful attitude toward Gentiles. A series of objections and false conclusions are raised in chapters 6–11, i.e., 6:1, 15; 7:7, 13; 9:14, 19; 11:1, 11, 19. These false inferences which pose possible objections to Paul's line of argument are usually rejected with "by no means!" *(mē genoito)* and then reasons are given for the rejection. Address in the second person singular to imaginary interlocutors also occur in 2:1–5; 9:19–21; 1:17–24; 14:4, 10. As in the diatribe, Paul uses censorious rhetorical questions, the expression "O man," and other typical elements of such apostrophes. The address in 11:17–24 is to a Gentile interlocutor who boasts over Jews. Paul also employs a number of other rhetorical features typical of the diatribe including virtue and vice lists, pesonification, comparisons, examples and rhetorical questions. His use of scripture differs in several respects from the diatribal quotation of authorities.

The methods of the diatribe are not of such central importance to any of Paul's other letters although the style appears at various places. In I Cor. 6:12–20, for example, Paul dialogues with a sloganeering interlocutor. Many diatribal features are clustered in 1 Cor. 15:29–35: rhetorical questions, direct address and exhortation to the audience, a proverbial saying, a quotation from the poet Menander, a question from an imaginary objector, censorious address to the objector, a comparison. In addition Paul uses the metaphor of fighting the wild beasts which was used by philosophers for the struggle with their passions.

In the past, Paul's dialogical language has been understood to be polemical. Commentators have read several diatribal texts (e.g. 2:17–29) as attacks on Judaism and its supposed legalism. The dialogical style, however, is pedagogical and hortatory rather than polemical. It is motivated by concern rather than contempt. It is also a misunderstanding to read dialogical features (e.g. objections) as references to actual groups in the Roman church.

The hortatory letter of James employs both themes and rhetorical techniques of the diatribe. These include indicting rhetorical questions, dramatic characterization, objections of an interlocutor, censorious address to an interlocutor, examples, comparisons, quotations, the motifs of the control of the tongue, word versus deed and the censure of pretentiousness. In James, as in other writings, it is not the occurrence of isolated stylistic phenomenon but the combination of multiple features in typical ways which permits the identification of the style as diatribal.

The style of the diatribe was employed by many later Christian writers and in Christian preaching. In second century North Africa, Tertullian employed the style with vigor. Clement of Alexandria quotes large portions of Musonius Rufus' diatribes almost verbatim. In the fourth century, Basil and especially Gregory Nazianzus reflect not only the highest philosophical and rhetorical training but also the themes and stylistic methods of the diatribe in many of their works. John Chrysostom and Asterius of Amasia very effectively acculturated the style and themes of the diatribe to the rhetoric of their sermons.

V. Annoted Bibliography

The most recent major work on the diatribe and also a discussion of its significance for Paul's letter to the Romans is Stanley K. Stowers, *The Diatribe and Paul's Letter to the Romans* (SBLDS 57; Chico, Cal.: Scholars Press, 1981). This book also contains extensive bibliography. The now dated classic work on Paul and the Diatribe is Rudolf Bultmann's, *Der Stil der paulinischen Predigt und die kynisch-stoische Diatribe* (FRLANT 13; Göttingen: Vandenhoeck & Ruprecht, 1910). For a critical discussion of work on the diatribe, especially among New Testament scholars, up to about 1970 see Abraham J. Malherbe, "Hellenistic Moralists and the New Testament." *Aufstieg und Niedergang der römischen Welt*, pt. 2, vol. 27, ed. Wolfgang Haase and Hildegard Temporini (Berlin; DeGruyter, forthcoming).

For the ancient meaning of *diatribē*, the work by Otto Halbauer is still very important: *De Diatribis Epicteti* (Diss. Leipzig, 1911). Halbauer's generic distinctions do not entirely hold up but his discussion of the subject is still useful. On the ancient meaning of *diatribē* see also John Glucker, *Antiochus and the Late Academy* (Hypomnemata 56; Göttingen: Vandenhoeck & Ruprecht, 1978) 159–166. Joseph Souilhe provides an excellent discussion of the diatribe and its school setting in Epictetus: *Épictète Entretiens* (Collection des universites de France; Paris: Société D'Édition "Les Belles lettres", 1975) 1. XX–XLII. A good survey of the history and style of the diatribe in pagan, Jewish and Christian authors with bibliography is Wilhelm Capelle and Henri Marrou, "Diatribe", *Reallexikon für Antike und Christentum* 3(1957) 990–1009. For the Epistle of James and Tertullian see Johannes Geffcken, *Kynika und Verwandtes* (Heidelberg: C. Winter, 1909).

CHAPTER 5
ANCIENT GREEK LETTERS

John L. White
Loyola University of Chicago

I. Introduction

The primary purpose of this essay is to describe the Christian letter tradition found in the New Testament and Early Church Fathers. In order to provide a proper setting for this description it will prove helpful to discuss ancient letter writing in general and then ancient Greek letter writing in particular. The examination of Greek letter writing is the largest part of the essay. Four specific types of letter are illustrated as a basis for considering the basic purposes which Greek letters served and, then, as a means for determining whether Christian letters have identifiable features that differentiate them from other Greek letters. The focus will be on Paul and how he wrote letters when, in the later part of the essay, we turn to describe the distinctive character of the Christian letter tradition.

A. *Letter Writing in Antiquity*
The discovery of vast numbers of letters within the last century shows that the letter was a common form of communication in biblical times. Letter writing was even more common than these archaeological finds show, because only letters written on decay-resistant materials or those preserved by a dry climate have survived.

Letter writing seems to have originated in various kinds of official correspondence between and within ancient states. Letters to and from kings, called Royal or Diplomatic correspondence, is the primary kind of Old Testament letter. Solomon's correspondence with King Hiram of Tyre is typical (1 Kgs 5:2–6 and 5:8–9. See 2 Chron 2:3–10 and 2:11–15). Military reports and orders constitute another category of ancient official

[1] See Yigael Yadin's analysis, "The Lachish Letters—Originals or Copies and Drafts?" pp. 179–86 of *Recent Archaeology in the Land of Israel*, ed. Hershel Shanks.

communication. The Lachish letters, written when Judah was being besieged by Babylonia, belong to this category.[1]

Another use to which ancient states put letter writing was the management of internal affairs. Hundreds of administrative letters between superiors and subordinates, from all levels of the bureaucratic structure, survive from Greco-Roman Egypt.[2]

B. The Development of Letter Writing

Though the letter was used relatively early by scholars in ancient Mesopotamia as a medium in which to express their ideas, for the most part the letter was only gradually adapted to "non-official" purposes. The adaptation was aided in Greco-Roman Egypt by the availability and relatively inexpensive cost of papyrus as a writing material.

Though most Greco-Roman papyrus letters of a private nature were written because of some specific need, especially of a business nature, a number have survived which were written for the more general purpose of maintaining family ties. When expressed in a cultivated manner, Greek and Roman rhetoricians regarded this use of the letter as the most authentic form of correspondence. For example, Cicero distinguished the letter as a cultivated expression of friendship from an ordinary letter occasioned by necessity in the following way: "That there are many kinds of letters you are well aware; there is one kind, however, about which there can be no mistake, for indeed letter writing was invented just in order that we might inform those at a distance if there were anything which it was important for them or for ourselves that they should know. A letter of this kind you will of course not expect from me."[3]

Though ancient epistolary theorists regarded the letter as a substitute for one's actual conversation and presence, they recognized that the letter had to be more articulate and studied than actual conversation because, like spoken conversation, a letter was subject to misunderstanding. And, in the case of the letter, the correspondent could not ask for immediate clarification. Consequently, though naturalness was important to letter writing, clarity was even more essential. In keeping with the conversational character of letter writing, the theorists advised against using the affected style of an orator and against using the letter for the exposition of a technical subject.[4]

---

[2] For a description of administrative letters, see pages 193, 198, and 200 in John L. White, *Light From Ancient Letters*.

[3] Cicero, *Letters*, 2.4.1. (pp. 100–101 in W. Glynn Williams, *Cicero. The Letters to his Friends*, vol. 1).

[4] See the comments to this effect in sections 225 and 230–32 of W. Rhys Roberts, *Demetrius: On Style*.

Despite the theorists injunctions against using the letter to write "speeches" about subjects artificial to actual conversation, epistolary treatises and letter essays increased steadily in later antiquity. And, in many case, these letters of instruction should not be regarded as so artificial as the theorists alleged. Much popular philosophy was dialogical in nature. Cynic-Stoic teaching used *diatribe*, for example, to instruct the populace, quoting phrases of an imaginary opponent which they then refuted in a series of questions and answers.[5] Though not so dialogical as the diatribe, the oral discourse (Greek: *homilia;* Latin: *(disputatio)* also had certain affinities with the oral character of the letter.

C. Oral Messages and Ancient Postal Service

Correspondence beteen ancient people originated as oral messages carried by couriers. We have evidence, both from Mesopotamia and from Israel (the Old Testament) that with the passage of time the message of the letter began to be delivered in written form, even though the sender of the letter was still identified orally at the beginning with the messenger formula, "Thus says . . ." David's letter to his military commander Joab was obviously written, and probably sealed, since it carried the order for the letter carrier's own death (2 Sam 11:14–15).

Eventually, even the sender's name was written and it continued to be placed at the beginning of the letter as it had been in oral messages. In a few cases the opening address and salutation continued to be delivered orally. For example, many Greco-Roman invitations contain only the details of the invitation itself and do not identify the sender and recipient. It is clear in this kind of situation that the messenger would have greeted the recipient orally.[6] The invitations in the Parable of the Great Supper would have been of the same type (Luke 14:15–24; Matt 22:1–10).

And, if the messenger had some special status or relation to the correspondents he might supplement the written message with an oral report even in other kinds of letters. The role of the courier is evident in the Apostle Paul's correspondence. It is clear that he relied on his trusted representatives to supplement what he had sent in the letter. The significance of the messenger to ancient correspondence may be illustrated by a brief description of ancient postal service.

The first organized postal system was introduced by the Persians in the sixth century B.C.E., when Cyrus set up a pony express system to manage his vast empire. The Persian post served as a model, first for

---

[5] See Rudolf Bultmann's analysis of the dialogical element in Paul's letters, which he compares with Cynic-Stoic diatribe, in his book, *Der Stil der paulinischen Predigt,* pp. 2–12, 64–71.

[6] See the analysis of invitations by Chan-Hie Kim, "The Papyrus Invitation," *JBL* 94 (1975), 391–402.

Alexander the Great and his successors and, later, for Augustus and the Roman Empire. Augustus introduced a number of refinements into the postal system, known as the *cursus publicus*, such as mile markers, inns, etc.[7]

The postal service described above was an effective system but, unfortunately for private citizens, it was created by rulers only to serve official business, namely, to carry military dispatches or diplomatic correspondence and to serve various administrative purposes within a state. Though the wealthy could use trusted slaves or employees as couriers, the average letter writer was dependent on travelling businessmen (e.g., passing caravans) or friends and passing strangers who happened to be travelling in the same direction as the letter. As one might expect, the latter form of postal service was often ineffective and unreliable, especially when parcel post was concerned.[8]

II. The Classification of Letters

The following explanation by Nils Dahl indicates why the classification of letters is not a simple matter: "Letters can be classified according to several criteria which often overlap: writing materials; mode of preservation; private, official, or public character; level of style; and what was most important to ancient letter theory—occasion, scope, and mood."[9]

Despite these difficulties in classification, there are identifiable Greek letters with fixed formal patterns and stereotyped phrases which constitute specific epistolary types. It will prove useful to illustrate some of these letters as a basis for talking more broadly about the purposes served by letter writing and about general formal features of letters. The following are illustrated and discussed below: Letters of introduction and recommendation, petitions, family letters, and royal letters of diplomacy.

A. *Letters of Introduction and Recommendation*

The three major divisions in a letter of recommendation, the opening, body, and closing, are clearly marked below. Identifiable divisions within the body are set off by double slash marks.[10]

---

[7] See W. L. Westermann, "On Inland Transportation and Communication," *Political Science Quarterly* 43 (1928), 364–87; M. Rostovtzeff. "Angariae," *Klio* 6 (1906), 249–58; and "Postal Service," p. 325 in *Oxford Classical Dictionary*, 2nd ed.

[8] See the examples cited in J. L. White, *Light from Ancient Letters*, 215.

[9] Dahl, "Letter," p. 539 in *Interpreter's Dictionary of the Bible*, Supplementary Volume (ed. Keith Crim).

[10] This letter is document 62 in *A Descriptive Catalogue of the Greek Papyri in the Collection of Wilfred Merton*, vol. 2, edited by B. R. Rees, H. I. Bell, and J. W. B. Barns. Its date is 6 CE.

Opening
Apollonios to Sarapion, the strategos and gymnasiarch, many greetings and continual good health.

Body
Isidoros, who carries this letter to you, is a member of my household. // Please regard him as recommended and, about whatever he should approach you, do it for him on my account. // By doing this (for me), I shall be favored by you. Moreover, in turn, you must indicate whatever you should want, and I shall act accordingly without hesitation.

Closing
Take care of yourself to stay well. Good-bye *(erroso)*. (Year) 36 of Caesar, Phaophi 26.

Letters of introduction and recommendation were identified as a specific type by ancient epistolary theorists. Two modern scholars, Clinton Keyes and Chan-Hie Kim, have described their stylistic and formal features in some detail.[11]

The form of the address/greeting (salutation) in the letter's opening is like that of most ordinary Greek letters of antiquity. Namely, "A (=the sender) to B (=the recipient) greeting." And, like many familial type letters a wish for health is joined directly to the opening salutation. Similarly, in the letter's closing the ordinary word of farewell *(erroso)* is used, followed by the date. A closing wish for health is expressed immediately prior to the farewell. In summary, the opening and closing of letters of recommendation are not especially distinctive but are like most letters written between friends, family members, and peers.

By contrast with the letter's opening and closing, the body of the letter is quite distinct and consists of a combination of features that is characteristic of letters of recommendation over several centuries. The introductory phrase identifies the person being recommended (the letter carrier) and/or his relation to the sender. Namely, "Isidoros, who carries this letter to you, is a member of my household." This stereotyped feature is followed, as indicated by the double slash marks, by the sender's recommendation (request) on the letter bearer's behalf: "Please regard him as recommended and, about whatever he should approach you, do it for him on my account." The third and final formal feature of the body is the letter writer's statement that he will be favored if the

---

[11] See C. W. Keyes, "The Greek Letter of Introduction," *American Journal of Philology* 56 (1935), 28–44 and Chan-Hie Kim, *The Familiar Letter of Recommendation* (1972).

recipient assists the letter carrier and by the sender's promise to repay the favor: "By doing this (for me), I shall be favored by you. Moreover, in turn, you must indicate whatever you should want, and I shall act accordingly without hesitation."

B. Letters of Petition

A letter of petition from the late third century B.C.E. is quoted below. The conventional parts of the body are identified, as they were in the letter of recommendation, by the double slash marks.[12]

Opening

To King Ptolemy, greetings from Philistia, daughter of Lysias, resident in Trikomia.

Body

I am wronged by Petechon. For as I was bathing in the baths of the aforesaid village, on Tybi 7 of the year 1, and had stepped out to soap myself he, being bathman in the women's rotunda and having brought in the jugs of hot water, emptied one over me and scalded my belly and my left thigh down to the knee, so that my life was in danger. On finding him, I gave him into the custody of Nechthosiris, the chief policeman of the village, in the presence of Simon the epistates. // I beg you therefore, O king, if it pleases you, as a suppliant who has sought your protection, not to suffer me, who am a working woman to be treated so lawlessly, but to order Diophanes the strategos to instruct Simon the epistates and Nechthosiris the policeman to bring Petechon before him that Diophanes may inquire into the case, // hoping that, having sought your protection, O king, the common benefactor, I may obtain justice.

Closing

Farewell (*eutuchei*).
Docket of instruction in a second hand: To Simon. Send the accused.

The essential function of the petition, like the letter of recommendation, is to request something of the recipient. The similarity of function is expressed in an analogous three-part structure in the body of the two letters. First, in both cases, the occasion of the request initiates the body and provides an explanation of the request. The content of the introductory statement varies in the petition of course from that in the letter of recommendation. In the present letter, for example, the petitioner iden-

---

[12]This is document 32 in O. Gueraud's collection of petitions, *ENTEYHEIS. Requetes et plaintes addresses au Roi d'Egypte*. Its date is 220 BCE.

tifies a specific person who has wronged her. In addition to this type of introductory statement, the petitioner may refer more obliquely to the circumstances which necessitate the request. Following this "background" statement, and analogous once again to the letter of recommendation, the petitioner states the request itself. In the present letter, the petitioner requests the king to rectify the situation. In many petitions, a lower official is requested to attend to the matter. Finally, the petitioner closes the request and the body by stating that she will be benefitted and justice accomplished by the king's favorable response to her request. In this case, too, the petition is comparable to the letter of recommendation, where the writer expresses appreciation to the recipient for attending to a requested matter.

In summary, the internal structure of the petition parallels the tripartite body of the letter of recommendation. In both, the sender initiates the body by reciting the circumstance(s) ("background") of the request. And, following the request itself, the sender acknowledges in both cases that he or she will be benefitted by the recipient's favorable response.

Despite the essential smiliarity of function and structure of the two letters of request, the relative status of the correspondents is quite different in the two cases. Whereas the author of the letter of recommendation writes as an equal, the petitioner writes from a position of inferiority. The petitioner's inferior status is reflected formally in the letter's opening. The petitioner places the recipient's name before her own in the form, "To B (the recipient), greetings from A (the sender)." Consequently, this form of letter opening is characteristic of petitions. The nature of the petitioner's relation to the recipient, an inferior writing to a superior about some grievance, was a deterant to expressions of familiarity, cordiality, and equality. It is for this reason that one never finds either an opening or concluding wish of health in letters of petition. And, just as petitioners always wrote the recipient's name before their own in the address, so too they always wrote *eutuchei* (*dieutuchei* in the Roman period) as the word of farewell. This closing formula differs from the ordinary word of farewell, *erroso*, which was used above in the letter of recommendation.

C. *Family Letters*

The following letter is from a young recruit to his mother in the second century C.E.[13] The young man, only recently inducted into the Roman fleet, informs his mother of safe arrival in Italy and in a postcript reports on his assignment to the fleet at Misenum. Since the opening and

---

[13] This is document 490 in *Papyri and Ostraca from Laranis*, edited by H. C. Youtie and J. G. Winter. It was written in the second century CE.

closing of family letters are more distinctive than their body, the isolable conventions are identified at the beginning and end of the letter (rather than in the body) by means of double slash marks. The description of Family letters which follows the letter is based on Heikki Koskenniemi's extensive research on Greco-Roman papyryus letters discovered in Egypt.[14]

Opening

Apollinarios to his mother, Taesion, many greetings. // Before all else I wish that you are well, // making obeisance on your behalf to all the gods. // And when I found someone who was journeying to you from Cyrene, I thought it a necessity to inform you about my welfare; you must inform me at once, in turn, about your safety and that of my brothers.

Body

And now I am writing to you from Portus, for I have not yet gone up to Rome and been assigned. When I am assigned and know where I will be, I will tell you immediately; and, for your part, do not hesitate to write about your welfare and that of my brothers. If you do not find someone coming to me, write to Socrates and he will transmit it to me.

Closing

I greet (salute) my brothers much, and Apollinarios and his children, and Kalalas and his children, and all your friends. Asklepiades salutes you. // I pray that you are well. I arrived in Portus on Pachon 25. (Postscript in a second hand:) Know that I have been assigned to Misenum, for I found out later (i.e., after the rest of the letter had been written).

Letters between family members, as the present letter illustrates, identify the recipient in the opening address with some familial description, e.g., "mother," "father," "brother" and "sister." The designation "lady" or "lord" is often applied respectively to the sender's mother and father. It is also common, as here, to expand the opening greetings with the qualification "much" (*pleista*) or "many" (*polla*). Similarly, almost all family letters express the wish for health in the letter's opening or closing and, often, in both places.

In addition to the preceding conventions in the letter's opening, the sender of a family letter often extends the health wish by stating that he

---

[14] H. Koskenniemi, *Studien zur Idee und Phraseologie des griechischen Briefes bis 400 n. Chr.*, 104–14.

praying on the recipient's behalf. Koskenniemi calls this the *proskynema* formula, because of the word for "obeisance" which is customarily used in making supplication to the god(s). He states that the convention arose in Egyptian religious circles, especially in connection with the god Sarapis, and that it was taken up into Greek letter writing by the Roman period.[15] Most often, as in the present example, the prayer is combined syntactically with the health wish and extends its sentiment by including the religious dimension.

In the letter closing, it is customary for Greek letters from Egypt to express extensive salutations to or from third parties. Also common, at least in the Roman era, is a closing wish for health which replaces the word of farewell that was customary in the Ptolemaic period. The word of farewell is itself a truncated expression of health.

Though one may talk as if the body of the family letter were a separate division, almost everything discussed in the middle of the letter is an extension of the correspondents' interest in each other's welfare. Koskenniemi concludes that, since there is no isolable message apart from the correspondents' interest in each other's welfare, family letters fail to take advantage of the full potential of the letter.[16] Note in the letter opening of the letter above that, after expressing a wish and prayer for his mother's welfare, the sender then informs his mother that he himself is well. He requests his mother, in turn, to write to him about her welfare and that of his brothers. And, though I suggest that the material which follows belongs to the body, one can easily see that it too is actually only an extension of the correspondents' interest in each other's well being and safety.

Assuming that one or another extension of the health wish qualifies as the message (body) of family correspondence, the following subjects come to expression in the body of such letters. Joy over receipt of a letter and complaint about the recipient's failure to write are frequent subjects, both of which imply an interest in information about family members and, in particular, in news about their welfare. Similarly, as in the letter above, the sender sometimes requests the recipient explicitly to write about family members' welfare.

D. Royal Correspondence

C. B. Welles made a collection of seventy-five royal letters, principally from the Seleucid and Attalid kingdoms.[17] Almost all were written by royal chancery secretaries and were sent to foreign city states where they were inscribed on stone after delivery. Some were initiated

---

[15] Koskenniemi 113ff.
[16] Koskenniemi 110f.
[17] Welles, *Royal Correspondence in the Hellenistic Period*.

by the king himself, others were written in response to an oral or written request from the foreign states.

The following letter was sent by Ptolemy II to Miletus in 262/1 BCE. The occasion of the correspondence was the imminent prospect that the Ptolemies would lose control of Miletus.[18] Major, isolable sections of the body are indicated once again with double slash marks.

Opening

King Ptolemy to the council and the people in Miletus, greeting.

Body

I have in former times shown all zeal in behalf of your city both through a gift of land and through care in all other matters as was proper because I saw that our father was kindly disposed toward the city and was the author of many benefits for you and had relieved you of harsh and oppressive taxes and tolls which certain of the kings had imposed. // Now also, as you guard steadfastly your city and our friendship and alliance—for my son and Callicrates and the other friends who are with you have written me what a demonstration you have made of good-will toward us—we knowing these things praise you highly and shall try to requite your people through benefactions, and we summon you for the future to maintain the same policy of friendship toward us so that in view of your faithfulness we may exercise even more our care for the city.

Closing

We have ordered Hegestratus to address you at greater length on these subjects and to give you our greeting. Farewell.

Regarding the formal characteristics of the royal letters inscribed on stone, Welles suggests that they may be divided generally into two groups, those which consist of a statement alone, and those which add an order to the statement.[19]

The latter type is based on the form of a private letter and it is customarily addressed to an individual rather than to a city. In its simplest form, the letter consists of a bare statement of the king's decision and his order, also without accompanying explanation. But the king may supplement this simple structure, at the beginning of the letter, by providing a rationale for his decision.

The second kind of royal letter, which was addressed to dependent

---

[18] This is document 14 in the aforementioned collection of C. B. Welles.
[19] See Welles' comments on pp. xlii–xlv.

city states, is based on the city decree which was the prevailing form of communication between communities. Like decrees, this type of letter consists of one long sentence or statement in two parts. An extensive statement, formed by a series of small parallel clauses, sets out the circumstances which occasion the king's decision. This long statement climaxes in the king's decision. Stated abstractly, the statement reads as follows: "Because of such-and-such circumstances we have decided the following."

The present letter to Miletus belongs to the second type of royal correspondence. It is an unusual example, however, because neither the occasion of the letter nor the king's decision are stated directly. Initially, Ptolemy II describes the kinds of sustained benefaction which both he and his father had granted to the city. After setting out these circumstances, Ptolemy praises the city for its appreciation of these benefactions and he exhorts it to maintain its loyalty in the future. The latter part of this long statement is obviously an implied request. Namely, the city was supposed to respond with a resolution of continued loyalty, as it in fact did. This type of letter, then, like certain other royal letters, is a kind of hybrid, on the borderline between the statement and the request. It is common in such correspondence for the sender to promise to reciprocate with a favor if the recipient complies with the request. In this respect, then, the tripartite structure—background, request, promise to repay the favor—is analogous to the structure in letters of recommendation and petition.

III. General Epistolary Functions and Structure

Most Greek letters are less specific in function than the letters illustrated above but, from the study of such correspondence, we may identify the three broad purposes which come to expression in letters. Namely, they: (1) convey information; (2) make requests or give commands/instructions; and (3) enhance or maintain personal contact with recipients. Each of these purposes is colored by the relative status of the sender to the recipient. For example, we saw how the request in the letter of recommendation differed from the entreaty in the letter of petition.

When one tries to determine which of the aforementioned purposes is intended in a letter, the determination ought not to be based on one or two stereotyped phrases within the letter. For example, the sender may introduce the body of the letter with an informational phrase (e.g., "I want you to know that . . .") and then proceed to request something of the recipient. Perhaps the letter serves two separate purposes, information and request. On the other hand, the initial disclosure of information may merely provide a rationale for the request which follows. Consequently, one ought to ascertain the logical relationship of conventions to each other and then determine the purpose of the letter on that basis.

Even more essential to the understanding of epistolary function is the recognition that there is a correlation between the three basic epistolary functions and the basic structure of the letter. Namely, the staying-in-touch aspect of letter writing is conveyed primarily through conventions which open or conclude the letter. On the other hand, the more specific occasions of the letter, identified as the disclosure of information and request or command, come to expression primarily in conventions used in the letter's body. Consequently, if the letter has a full opening and closing, the sender's primary intent is to say in touch with the recipient and the correspondence is a family letter or a letter of friendship. By contrast, if the body is full and the opening and closing are minimal, the letter is motivated by some more specific purpose than the maintenance of contact.

IV. Greek Letter Writing and the Christian Letter Tradition

A. *Comparing the Christian and Greek Letters*

With few exceptions, Christian letters are longer than ordinary Greek letters. To be sure, some Greek letters are three to four times the length of the representative letters illustrated above. Nonetheless, the New Testament and Patristic letters tend to be longer than even the longest examples. Their length is to be explained in large part by their purpose as letters of instruction.

Their combination of parts also tends to be more diversified than most letters. Thus, so far as structure is concerned, they are reminiscient of the Synoptic Gospels in the way other genres are combined within an outer frame. Lists of vices and virtues, lists of duties for members of the household, doxologies, benedictions, and other prayer formulas are among the materials included in Christian letters.

With respect to their epistolary setting, Christian letters are akin to royal letters in being addressed to communities and like philosophical letters which were addressed to a community of students. In their didactic interests they may also be compared with philosophical letters of instruction. So far as emotional tone or mood is concerned, they are more like familial letters between equals than orders to subordinates.

B. *Paul the Letter Writer*

The following abstracted outline of letter parts shows the features that are characteristic of Paul's correspondence. And they indicate, in turn, the nature of his relationship with the congregations which he founded as the Apostle to the Gentiles.

Opening
   Address: Paul, an apostle of Jesus Christ, to the church of God at _____, sanctified (beloved, called, etc.) in Christ.
   Grace greeting: Grace to you and peace from God our Father and the Lord Jesus Christ.
   Thanksgiving prayer: I thank God (always) for (all of) you, because of . . . , and I pray that the Lord may make you increase (mature) in such activity so that you may be pure and blameless when Christ returns.

Body
   Introductory formula: I want to know, brethren, that . . . (I/we do not want you to be ignorant, brethren, that/of . . .). Or: I appeal to you, brethren, that . . .
   Transitional formulas: Often indicated by Paul's use of the vocative, "brethren," and with request/disclosure phrases.
   Concluding section/Paul's Apostolic Presence section
      1. Autobiographical (authoritative) reference to the letter and expression of confidence in the recipients' willingness to comply with Paul's instruction.
      2. Identification/recommendation of Paul's messenger.
      3. Announcement of Paul's anticipated (hoped for) visit.
      4. Parenetic section: Reminder of Paul's instruction, reference to Paul's/the congregation's former conduct, appeal to the example of Christ.
      5. Prayer of Peace.

Closing
   Closing greetings: from (to) third parties
   The Holy Kiss greeting
   Grace benediction: the grace of our (the) Lord Jesus Christ be with you (your spirit).

There is nearly universal agreement that, of the thirteen letters attributed to Paul, he wrote at least seven: Romans, 1, 2 Corinthians, Galatians, Philippians, 1 Thessalonians and Philemon. The above outline is based on these seven letters. We will turn shortly to a more specific description of the way Paul wrote letters. In the meantime, the following comments will provide a general explanation of how and why Paul wrote letters.

Apart from Paul's letter to the Romans, and it may not finally prove an exception, all of his letters were occasioned by actual issues which, from his viewpoint, called for a specific response. Ideally, Paul would have preferred to address the issues in person but, since that was not always possible, the letter and/or the messenger became his substitute.

Since Paul wrote in his capacity as an apostle of Jesus Christ, his letters were always religious. Consequently, when Paul addressed his congregations, he imagined them at worship and himself as officiating at the service. It is for this reason that he combines epistolary conventions with the language of thanksgiving, blessing, and prayer, and why salutation is enjoined as a religious act (e.g., the holy kiss).

Though Paul wrote as leader of the congregation, the emotional tone of his correspondence is friendly and familial. This unusual combination of equality and authority calls for explanation. On the one hand, Paul addressed his recipients with the egalitarian designation, "brethren," because he and they had familial ties through common spiritual generation. Similarly, though Paul referred to his status as apostle in the opening address formula, he also referred to the elect status of his recipients with such designations as "saints," "called" (elect), "sanctified," and "beloved." However, on the other hand, Paul referred to himself as his recipients' spiritual father, as the steward of the household, a mother in labor, and a nurse; designations indicative of Paul's special responsibility within the family of faith. Consequently, though Paul and his congregations were familially related by God's grace, Paul had been assigned the responsibility of securing his brethren's spiritual maturation. The character of Paul's apostolicity may now be illustrated concretely with reference to the above outline.

Paul uses the common form of opening address in all seven letters, that in which the sender's name is written prior to the recipient's. But, for the single word of salutation, "greetings" *(chairein)*, he substitutes an independent grace greeting: "Grace to you and peace from God our Father and the Lord Jesus Christ." Paul nowhere expresses the customary wish for health but the grace greeting is its religious equivalent. Similarly, following the opening grace greeting, Paul expresses thanksgiving to God because he has learned of some spiritual activity of his recipients. Thereupon, he prays that his recipients' activity will result in their full spiritual maturation by Christ's return. Consequently, though Paul does not express the ordinary wish for health, he does convey concern for his recipients' welfare in the grace greeting and thanksgiving. And, in both cases, his concern in not with ordinary well-being but with his recipients' spiritual welfare, in his anticipation of the completion of the new age.

Conventions in the letter's closing also reflect the religious setting of Paul's correspondence. Thus, in a manner nearly identical to the opening greeting, Paul replaces the customary word of farewell with the following grace blessing: "The grace of our Lord Jesus Christ be with you (your spirit)." The closing greetings from people with Paul (third parties) to the recipients are similar to conventional practice. However, when Paul proceeds, on occasion, to exhort members of the congregation to greet each other with a holy kiss (1 Cor. 16:20b; 2 Cor. 13:12; 1 Thess. 5:26; Rom. 16:20), he departs from convention.

Generally speaking, the opening and closing of Paul's letters show that he is satisfied with his recipients and that he is intent on fostering the continuation of good relations. However, in the case of Galatians, thanksgiving gives way to an expression of dissatisfaction and astonishment, occasioned by the Galatians' decision to adopt a different set of religious commitments than those to which Paul himself was dedicated.

Regarding the body portion of Paul's letters, common features are less evident than in the opening and closing. The recurrence of major motifs, and of an identifiable structure, seems to be limited to the closing section of the body. So far as the introductory part of the body is concerned, Paul introduces the message with conventional epistolary phrases: a disclosure formula in five cases (Romans, 2 Corinthians, Galatians, Philippians and 1 Thessalonians) and a request formula in the two remaining letters (1 Corinthians and Philemon).

Though we cannot identify formal correspondences in the large section of the body between the introductory formula and the section which concludes the body, we can speak about the similarity of social setting which Paul envisioned as he wrote this part of the letter. The theological body is characterized by dialogical and argumentative features that are especially influenced by oral rhetorical traditions. The individual letters, or certain parts of them, reflect the influence of one or another type of argumentation. For example, hortatory reminder, and a parenetic style, characterizes 1 Thessalonians. Similarly, recommendation is an important aspect of Philemon, apology is a significant feature of Gal 1–2, 1 Cor 1–4 and 2 Cor 10–13. In short, Paul's conceived of the letter in every case as a written substitute for the oral delivery he would have spoken to the congregation if he could have actually been present.

In the above description of Greek epistolary types, we saw that phrases which close the body serve either to encourage the continuity of relationships (especially in family letters) or to finalize and/or underscore the occasion of the correspondence (e.g., in petitions and letters of recommendation). Paul uses some of the same techniques to conclude the letter's message but here too, as in his adaptation of opening and closing conventions, his own special sense of apostolic presence is communicated to his congregations.

Robert W. Funk has suggested in connection with this section of the letter, which he calls the "Apostolic *Parousia* (Presence)" section, that Paul indicated his reason for writing (item 1 above), his intention to dispatch an apostolic messenger (item 2), and his intention or desire to make a personal visit (item 3).[20] In practice, Funk notes that only two of these three aspects of Paul's apostolicity are actually expressed. Paul either emphasizes the apostolic character of the letter or he recommends the letter carrier to the congregation, but he does not refer to both on the same occasion. When a trusted messenger was available to represent him, Paul did not need to emphasize his role as the letter's sender. Contrariwise, when he could not send an apostolic courier, nor pay an immediate visit, he emphasized the importance of attending to his written instruction, i.e., "I Paul write (say) to you . . ."[21]

The fourth structural item at the end of the body of Paul's letters in his parenetic instruction. Commenting on Paul's purpose in reminding his recipients of the traditional instruction he had taught them, Nils A. Dahl has suggested that Paul conceived of his apostolic commission not only in terms of being an end-time herald to the Gentiles but also as being responsible for their spiritual maturation and holiness by Christ's return.[22] Thus, whereas the preceding aspects of Paul's apostolicity seem to address situational issues, the parenetic reminder and/or the appeal to the example of Christ, show why Paul is so concerned about his congregations' conduct. Paul is responsible for his recipients' progress toward the norms God has established in Christ for the new age. The projected outcome of their maturation is indicated by the prayer/statement of peace, with which Paul closes this section. The peace which Paul envisions is the end-time peace which God will consummate when Christ returns.

C. Other Christian Letter Traditions

In past studies I have emphasized that Paul's influence as an apostolic letter writer was the primary reason that twenty-one of the New Testament's documents are more or less in epistolary form. I now think that this explanation is probably too simple, even though his influence is clearly evident in the remaining letters attributed to him (i.e., 2 Thessalonians, Colossians, Ephesians, 1, 2 Timothy and Titus). Paul was also a model for Ignatius of Antioch and Polycarp, but they were influenced by other epistolary traditions as well.

Along with 2 and 3 John, Paul's letters are the most situational in the New Testament. Though didactic in purpose, ordinary epistolary considerations constitute an important part of the communication. But, in other Christian letters, the more ephemeral and personal aspects of letter

---

[20] Funk, "The Apostolic *Parousia:* Form and Significance," pp. 258–61 in *Christian History and Interpretation*, ed. W. R. Farmer *et. al.*

[21] Funk, pp. 258–61.

[22] Dahl makes this statement on p. 75 of an unpublished paper, "Paul's Letter to the Galatians: Epistolary Genre, Content, Structure" (presented at the 1973 annual meeting of the Society of Biblical Literature).

writing are largely excluded. They are largely replaced by enduring didactic instruction which transcends time and space. These New Testament letters derive from a different model than Paul's letters. Various philosophical letters of instruction may constitute a better parallel. The letter to the Hebrews is probably the purest New Testament example of a letter in which the same theme is sustained from beginning to end. 1 Peter is also influenced by such a tradition.

So far as the intent of other Christian letters is concerned, 1 Clement is a letter of advice; James was most influenced by traditional wisdom and parenesis; 2 Timothy and 2 Peter were conceived as literary testaments; and, analogous to philosophical instruction addressed to individual students, 1 Timothy and Titus contain advice for young ministers. Several New Testament letters are in the form of encyclicals and were intended to address a wider public (e.g., Acts 15:23; Rev 1:4–7; 1, 2 Peter; James).

V. Conclusion

The epistolary form was a very common genre in late antiquity and it served an almost limitless array of functions. In addition to private purposes, most of which were occasioned by specific need, there was a spectrum of diplomatic, military, and administrative purposes for which ancient states used letters. Petitions, applications, and contractual/legal documents in letter form constitute another large body of ancient correspondence. And, with the democratization of knowledge in late antiquity, it was almost inevitable that philosophical and religious instruction would be written eventually in epistolary form.

Though the Christian letter tradition is itself diverse and draws upon various epistolary models, there are certain common features which bear repeating or emphasizing here. They tend to be longer than most ancient letter and this results from their common purpose as letters of instruction. With few exceptions, they are apostolic communications or speeches addressed to a Christian community. Hence, they are authoritative pieces of correspondence, which appeal to scripture, revelation, and traditional instruction. By means of traditional theological instruction, theological argumentation and parenetic reminder they constituted an effective medium of persuasion for the guidance of the early church.

VI. Annotated Bibliography

A. *General Studies*

1. *Greek and Latin letter writing.*

The short essay, "Letters, Greek," by R. Hackforth and B. R. Rees in the *Oxford Classical Dictionary*, 2nd ed. (1970), is a good introductory study of Greek letter writing. It divides Greek letters into six general classes and discusses ancient theories about the purpose and style of letters. For Latin letter writing, readers should consult "Letters, Latin," by R. G. C. Levens, also in the *Oxford Classical Dictionary*, 2nd. ed. This essay discusses postal service, writing materials, the use of scribes in the Roman Empire and identifies major representatives of the Latin literary tradition.

A much longer study of ancient Greek letter writing was made by Heikki Koskenniemi, *Studien zur Idee und Phraseologie des griechischen Briefes bis 400 n. Chr.* (1956). Koskenniemi explains the general Greek conception of the letter's nature and purpose by means of ancient scholarly theories about letter writing and through studying recurring phrases in ancient non-literary letters written on papyrus. Klaus Thraede has also written a lengthy study of ancient Greek letter writing, *Grundzüge griechish römischer Brieftopik* (1970). Like Koskenniemi, Thraede sketches the ancient scholarly letter theory. However, he concentrates much more on the literary letter tradition in his analysis of actual letters. One may add to these two works the essay by Abraham J. Malherbe, "Ancient Epistolary Theorists," *Ohio Journal of Religious Studies* 5 (1977), 3–77. The essay contains an extensive collection of comments about the idea of the letter by ancient epistolary theorists.

For collections of Greek and Latin letters in translation, two recent publications are useful: Stanley K. Stowers, *Letter Writing in Greco-Roman Antiquity* (1986); and John L. White, *Light from Ancient Letters* (1986). Stowers' work includes a broad sampling of both non-literary and literary letters. My book contains a number of documentary (non-literary) letters from Greco-Roman Egypt, along with a lengthy essay on Greek letter writing and ancient postal service.

Three older collections of letters may be added to the above. Dorothy Brooke made a useful collection of Greek and Roman private letters from the fifth century BCE to the fifth century CE, *Private Letters Pagan and Christian (1930)*. Adolf Deissmann included twenty-six letters, with explanatory comments, in his collection of ancient documents, *Light from the Ancient East* (1910. repr. 1978. cf. pp. 149–251). In their *Select Papyri*, vols I (1932) and II (1934), A. S. Hunt and C. C. Edgar included a representative selection of private letters (texts 88–169 of vol. I) and administrative (official) correspondence (texts 409–434 of vol. II).

2. New Testament and Patristic Letters.

The essay by Nils A. Dahl, "Letter" (pp. 538–40 in *Interpreter's Dictionary of the Bible*, supplementary volume), is a useful discussion of issues relevant to the understanding of biblical letters. In addition to dealing with the oral stage of letters, the courier's role in the letter's message, and the general purposes served by letters, he compares biblical letters (especially NT letters) with their secular counterparts. William G. Doty's *Letters in Primitive Christianity* (1973) deals at greater length with the relation of Christian letter writing to Greco-Roman letters. Similar in scope is my own essay: J. L. White, "New Testament Epistolary Literature in the Framework of Ancient Epistolography," pp. 1730–56 in *Aufstieg und Niedergang der römischen Welt* 25.2 (1984).

B. *Special Studies*

1. *Greek Letters*

Ostensibly, the book by F. X. J. Exler, *The Form of the Ancient Greek Letter* (1923), is a study of the general form of various kinds of Greek letters on the basis of their epistolary formulas. In fact, the study is an analysis of conventions in the letter's opening and closing. Nonetheless, the book is a useful compendium of conventions (opening formulas of address, health wish conventions, etc.) in those two parts of the letter. A companion to Exler's work is my analysis of the letter's body: J. L. White, *The Body of the Greek Letter* (1972). Both studies concentrate on non-literary papyrus letters written in Greco-Roman Egypt. One ought to add to these two analyses Henry Steen's study of epistolary clichés. "Les Clichés épistolaries dans les Lettres sur Papyrus Grecques," *Classica et Mediaevalia* 1 (1938), 119–76. Steen differentiates clichés from formulas by suggesting that clichés are less functional and more ornamental.

2. *New Testament Letters*

Two groundbreaking English studies on the application of form critical principles to the study of New Testament letters are: Paul Schubert, "Form and Function of the Pauline Letter," *Journal of Religion* 19 (1939), 365–77; and Robert W. Funk, "The Letter: Form and Style," in *Language; Hermeneutic, and Word of God* (1966), 150–74. In Funk's essay, the cumulative result of numerous form critical studies on the individual segments of St. Paul's letters is sketched.

For the discussion of Greco-Roman rhetoric and epistolography (the literary letter tradition) in connection with St. Paul's letters, see Hans Dieter Betz, "The Literary Composition and Function of Galatians," in *Galatians* (1979), 14–25. We may add to Betz's use of rhetoric and epistolography to interpret Galatians William Schoedel's study of the same characteristics in his commentary, *Ignatius of Antioch* (1985), 7–8 (and frequently).

The following studies examine other specific segments or aspects of New Testament letter writing: K. Berger, "Apostelbrief und apostolische Rede, ZNW 65 (1974), 190–231; C. J. Bjerkelund, *Parakalô*, Bibliotheca Theologica Norvegica 1 (1967); F. O. Francis, "The Form and Function of the Opening and Closing Paragraphs of James and 1 John," *ZNW* 61 (1970), 110–26; R. W. Funk, "The Apostolic *Parousia*," *Christian History and Interpretation*, ed. W. R. Farmer *et. al.* (1967), 249–68, and "The Form and Structure of II and III John," *JBL* 86 (1967), 424–30; T. Y. Mullins, "Formulas in NT Epistles," *JBL* 91 (1972), 380–90, "Greeting as a NT Form," *JBL* 87 (1968), 418–26. "Disclosure: A Literary Form in the NT," *NovT* 5 (1964), 44–50, and "Petition as a Literary Form," *NovT* 5 (1962), 46–54; J. T. Sanders, "The Transition from Opening Epistolary Thanksgiving to Body in the Letters of the Pauline Corpus," *JBL* 81 (1962), 348–62; P. Schubert, *Form and Function of the Pauline Thanksgivings* (1939); S. K. Stowers, *The Diatribe and Paul's Letter to the Romans* (1981).

C. Epistolary Classes and Types

Two scholars have described the stylistic and formal features of ancient Greek letters of recommendation: Clinton W. Keyes, "The Greek Letter of Introduction," *American Journal of Philology* 56 (1935), 28–44; and Chan-Hie Kim, *The Familiar Letter of Recommendation* (1972). To these two works, we may add an analysis of Latin letters of recommendation by Hannah Cotton, *Documentary Letters of Recommendation* (1981).

The Cynic Epistles (1977. repr. 1986), by A. J. Malherbe, is a useful collection of pseudepigraphic epistles (philosophical/literary letters) attributed to representatives of Cynicism, including Anacharis, Crates, Diogenes, Heraclitus, and Socrates.

Though not all the documents are letters, the book by Robert Sherk, *Roman Documents from the Greek East* (1969), contains a number of official Roman letters from the period of the Roman Republic (especially texts 33–78). Similar in type to the letters in Sherk's collection, but written by Greek kingdoms to their dependences, are the letters collected by C. B. Welles, *Royal Correspondence in the Hellenistic Period* (1934).

A pioneering study of Greek letters of petition was made by O. Gueraud, *ENTEYHEIS. Requêtes et plaintes addresses au Roi d'Égypte au Ille siècle avant J. C.* (1931). More recently, a study was made by J. L. White, *The Form and Structure of the Official Petition* (1972). The latter work has an appendix of seventy-one petitions.

By means of stylistic features, Heikki Koskenniemi classified a number of Greek letters from Roman Egypt as "family letters" (see *Studien zur Idee*, 104–14). J. G. Winter identified letters from young soldiers (especially recent recruits) as a sub species of family letters in his little collection, "In the Service of Rome: Letters from the Michigan Collection of Papyri," *Classical Philology* 22 (1927), 237–56. In Paul Dion's comparative study of Greek and Aramaic family letters from

Egypt, "The Aramaic 'Family Letter'" (in *Semeia* 22, 59–76), he showed that the style of both Greek and Aramaic family letters was influenced by native Egyptian practice.

Chan-Hie Kim described stylistic features of letters of invitation in his essay, "The Papyrus Invitation," *JBL* 94 (1975), 391–402.

C. Ancient Postal Service

The book by Laurin Zilliacus, *From Pillar to Post* (1956) is a popular and engaging account of postal service in antiquity. W. L. Westerman wrote an informative account of the origin and early development of the ancient postal service in his essay, "On Inland Transportation and Communication in Antiquity," *Political Science Quarterly* 43 (1937–38), 270–87. The reader may find it useful also to consult the article, "Postal Service," in the *Oxford Classical Dictionary* (2nd ed.), 325.

CHAPTER 6
GRECO-ROMAN BIOGRAPHY

David E. Aune
Saint Xavier College

I. Introduction

Biography was one of the more complex and varied literary forms of antiquity. Though the Greek biographical tradition had its roots in the fifth century B.C., the actual term "biography" (Greek: *biographia*) first appears in the late fifth century A.D. Earlier authors generally referred to such works as "lives" (Greek: *bioi*; Latin: *vitae*). Greco-Roman biography is a type of independent literary composition which typically focused on the character, achievements and lasting significance of a memorable and exemplary individual from birth to death, emphasizing his public career. In Israelite and early Jewish literature, on the other hand, biography as an independent literary form is rarely attested and developed only very late (first century A.D.) and under Hellenistic influence.[1]

A. *Types of Greco-Roman Biography*

The most influential modern study of ancient biography has been Friedrich Leo's book *Die griechisch-römische Biographie nach ihrer litterarischen Form* ("Greco-Roman Biography According to Its Literary

---

[1] Using Hellenistic literary models, for example, Philo of Alexandria (ca. 30 B.C.E. to 45 C.E.) wrote biographies of Moses and the Patriarchs. In first century C.E. Palestine, the anonymous *Vitae Prophetarum* ("Lives of the Prophets") arose. This work consists of short biographical sketches of twenty-three Israelite prophets. For a discussion of Israelite-Jewish "biography" see David E. Aune, *The New Testament in Its Literary Environment* (Philadelphia: Westminster Press, 1987) 36–42, and Klaus Baltzer, *Die Biographie der Propheten* (Neukirchen-Vluyn: Neukirchener Verlag, 1975). On Philo, see Anton Priessnig, "Die literarische Form der Patriarchen-biographien des Philon von Alexandria," *Monatsschrift für Geschichte und Wissenschaft des Judentums* 37 (1929), 143–55. On the *Vitae Prophetarum*, see Charles C. Torrey, *The Lives of the Prophets: Greek Text and Translation* (Philadelphia: Society of Biblical Literature and Exegesis, 1946).

Form"), which appeared in 1901. Leo distinguished two major types of biography, Peripatetic biography (exemplified by Plutarch's *Lives*), and Alexandrian biography (exemplified by the *Lives of the Caesars* of Suetonius, and the *Lives of the Philosophers* of Diogenes Laertius). Both types originated with Artistotle and his school (called the Peripatetic school). Peripatetic biography is characterized by a chronological arrangement with literary pretensions. This type of biography was particularly suitable for presenting the lives of politicians, generals and philosophers, and the ruling assumption was that a person's character was revealed through his actions. Alexandrian biography, on the other hand, reportedly originated with the grammarians at the Museum at Alexandria who were also under the influence of Aristotle. This type of biography is characterized by topical and systematic arrangement, had no real literary pretensions, and was particularly appropriate for presenting the lives of famous artists and authors. These biographies were specifically designed as introductions to commentaries on, and summaries of, the works of famous literary figures. The two types of biography described by Leo were also recognized by Quintilian, the famous first century A.D. rhetorical teacher, as alternate approaches to encomium, i.e., a speech in praise of a person (*Institutes* 3.7.15; LCL translation):

> Praise awarded to character is always just, but may be given in various ways. It has sometimes proved the more effective course to trace a man's life and deeds in due chronological order, praising his natural gifts as a child, then his progress at school, and finally the whole course of his life, including words as well as deeds. At times on the other hand it is well to divide our praises, dealing separately with the various virtues, fortitude, justice, self-control and the rest of them and to assign to each virtue the deeds performed under its influence.

Often ancient writers combined both the chronological and topical approaches to the presentation of the life of a famous person. Xenophon's encomium *Agesilaus* begins with a chronological narrative of the deeds of Agesilaus (1–2), yet is dominated by a topical exposition of his virtues (3–11). The chronological tendency exhibited in Peripatetic biography probably originated in Hellenistic historiography with its largely chronological presentation of political and military matters within the framework of the war monograph (e.g., Herodotus, Thucydides), or the more comprehensive framework of universal history (e.g., Polybius). Alexandrian biography, on the other hand, owes much to the systematic discussions of antiquarians (e.g., Dionysius of Halicarnassus and Suetonius). Both the chronological and topical tendencies in ancient biography, however, are usually found together in many ancient biographies.

Since Leo's twofold ideal typology of Greco-Roman biography makes no accomodations for biographies in which features from both types are present, other scholars have proposed modifications and amplifications of Leo's scheme. Fritz Wehrli proposed a related typology consisting of three types of ancient biography with many mixed forms: (1) Biographies of philosopher's and poets (Leo's Peripatetic type), (2) Encomiastic-rhetorical biographies of statesmen and generals, (3) Short biographical sketches, particularly of famous authors.[2] Klaus Berger, building on both Leo and Wehrli, has proposed a fourfold typology: (1) The encomium type (Isocrates, *Evagoras*, Xenophon, *Agesilaus*, Philo, *Life of Moses* Tacitus, *Agricola*, Lucian, *In Praise of Demosthenes*), (2) The Peripatetic type, a chronological narrative of moral character exemplified by deeds (Plutarch), (3) The popular, novelistic type (Xenophon, *Cyropaedia;* the anonymous *Life of Aesop* and *Life of Secundus*), and (4) The Alexandrian type, systematically organized (Suetonius).[3] Both typologies, however, are unsatisfactory, since constituent categories are based on inconsistent generic criteria. Wehrli's appeal to "mixed types" reveals the difficult of any such typology. Recently Charles Talbert has proposed a typology based exclusively on five possible *functions* of biography: (1) to provide a pattern to copy, (2) to replace a false with a true image of the teacher worthy of emulation, (3) to discredit a teacher, (4) to indicate where authentic tradition is to be found, and (5) to validate or provide an interpretive key to a teacher's doctrine.[4] Yet this proposal is not fully satisfactory since it focuses on the *function* of biography to the exclusion of other important generic features. The development of a more satisfactory typology of Greco-Roman biography can only take place when a great many examples of this literary type have undergone detailed literary analysis. This task has yet to be achieved.

B. Major Features of Greco-Roman Biography

Greco-Roman biography, in contrast to its modern counterpart, was primarily focused on famous people as representative *types* (i.e., as representatives of group values) rather than as unique individuals.[5] The primary identity of ancient individuals was anchored in kinship groups (*genos,* "family," *phratria,* "clan," *phyle,* "tribe") as well as in larger

---

[2] Fritz Wehrli, "Gnome, Anekdote und Biographie," *Museum Helveticum,* 30 (1973), 194–208.

[3] Klaus Berger, "Hellenistische Gattungen im Neuen Testament," *Aufstieg und Niedergang der römischen Welt,* Part II, Vol. 25/2 (New York and Berlin: W. de Gruyter, 1984) 1231–43.

[4] Charles H. Talbert, *What is a Gospel? The Genre of the Canonical Gospels* (Philadelphia: Fortress Press, 1977) 92–93.

[5] Bruce J. Malina, *The New Testament World: Insights from Cultural Anthropology* (Atlanta: John Knox Press, 1981), devotes a chapter to "The First-Century Personality: The Individual and the Group" (pp. 51–70).

social and political units (oikos or *oikia,* "household," *eranos* or *thiasos,* "club," *demos,* "commune," *polis,* "city").⁶ Individual personalities were assumed to be as fixed and unchanging as the kinship groups and the social and political units within which they were enmeshed. Greco-Roman biographies, therefore, are more *idealistic* than *realistic.* Consequently, the subjects of most ancient biographies are depicted as static personalities presented as paradigms of either traditional virtues or vices, rarely as a mixture of both. There are several features of ancient biography which can be correlated with this emphasis on the typical and the ideal. First the subjects thought most suitable for biographical description were men prominent in public life (i.e., those active in the assembly, the market place, the gymnasium, the theater, the battlefield, and the law court) whose lives appropriately reflected the norms and values of the state (e.g., generals, politicians, kings, philosophers, poets, orators). Second, the chronological framework used in ancient biography was the means of organizing the external facts of the subject's life, not for tracing the development of his personality (which was assumed to be static). Third, the idealistic approach to biographical writing combined with the rhetorical purpose in portraying the subject as a model of virtue inevitably led to distortion and the inclusion of an indeterminate amount of fictional elements.

Greco-Roman biography is an *inclusive* literary form which provides a framework or setting for various types of short forms including anecdotes (which Greek rhetoricians called *chreiai*), maxims *(gnomai),* and reminiscences *(apomnemoneumata). Chreiai* are essentially sayings or actions (or a combination of the two) set in a brief narrative framework (e.g., the question-and-answer section of the *Life of Secundus*).⁷ *Gnomai* are proverbial sayings which lack attribution or a narrative framework, and *apomnemoneumata* are expanded *chreiai* thought to be transmitted by memory. Examples of longer literary forms which can be included in biographies are novellas, speeches and dialogues (as in the *Life of Secundus*).

II. Text: Secundus the Silent Philosopher

A. Introduction

The anonymous life of Secundus the philosopher was a popular literary composition originally written in Greek toward the end of the

---

⁶S. C. Humphreys, "Kinship in Greek Society, c. 800–300 B.C.," *Anthropology and the Greeks* (London: Routledge & Kegan Paul, 1978) 193–208; *idem,* "*Oikos* and *Polis*," *The Family, Women and Death* (London: Routledge & Kegan Paul, 1983) 1–21. W. K. Lacey *The Family in Classical Greece* (Ithaca: Cornell University Press, 1968).

⁷See the detailed discussion of *chreiai* in the essay by Vernon K. Robbins included in this volume.

second century A.D. The work was widely disseminated during the medieval period and was translated (and amplified) in Latin, Syriac, Armenian, Arabic, and Ethiopic. The exact identity of this philosopher is unknown, though there was a second century Athenian sophist or rhetorician named Secundus, a teacher of Herodes Atticus (Philostratus *Lives of the Sophists* 1.26; 2.1). "Secundus" (originally meaning "second born") was a common Roman cognomen or family name during the imperial period, and it is quite possible that there was a second-century philosopher with the name Secundus, contemporary with Hadrian (A.D. 117–138), unknown from any other source.

The *Life of Secundus* is a type of biography which has no close literary parallels in Greco-Roman literature. To that extent it is *unique*. Since very few popular biographies have survived from Greco-Roman antiquity, the judgment that the *Life of Secundus* is unique rests uneasily on the argument from silence. Yet the *Life of Secundus* is composed of four major sections, each of which consists of a particular literary form which has many ancient literary parallels. If the whole is distinctive, the parts are certainly not.

The first section is a *novella* which provides the reason why Secundus maintained the life-long practice of silence by narrating the fateful reunion of Secundus with his mother.[8] Novellas (or romantic tales) are short stories narrating the resolution of a dramatic tension. While novellas often consist in a single episode, they may include several. They were never fully independent literary forms, but were placed in collections (e.g., Aristides, *Milesian Stories*), or inserted in such inclusive literary forms as dialogues (Lucian *Toxaris*, contains ten short stories illustrating friendship), in histories as digressions (e.g. Herodotus 2.121, the novella of the Clever Thief with three episodes) and novels (e.g. In Apuleius, *The Golden Ass*, fifteen novellas, constituting 60% of the text, are inserted at various points in the narrative).[9] Novellas, like the one in the *Life of Secundus*, often center on erotic themes. This one is constructed around the theme of the man who, after a lengthy time away, returns home incognito to test members of his household (including the folklore motifs

---

[8] See Sophie Trenker, *The Greek Novella in the Classical Period* (Cambridge: University Press, 1958); Ben E. Perry, *The Ancient Romances* (Berkeley: University of California Press, 1967) 79–84. Martin Dibelius has an extensive discussion of the Greek novella, or tale, in *From Tradition to Gospel* (New York: Charles Scribner's Sons, n.d.), 164–72. Unfortunately, his discussion is weakened because he confounds the novella with the ancient miracle story. The two forms are quite different in both history and content. Mark 6:17–29, the story of the imprisonment and death of John the Baptist, is a novella.

[9] On Herodotus see W. Aly, *Volksmärchen, Sage und Novelle bei Herodot und seinen Zeitgenossen* (Göttingen, 1921); on Apuleius see the perceptive study by John J. Winkler, *Auctor & Actor: A Narratological Reading of Apuleius's "The Golden Ass"* (Berkeley: University of California Press, 1985).

of the chastity test and the recognition scene). In Greek literature this theme first occurs in the Odyssey, where Penelope proves true to her long-absent husband, as do Telemachus and a handful of servants. In the *Life of Secundus* his mother fails the test and commits suicide.

The second section focuses on the testing of the resolve of Secundus by the emperor Hadrian, who threatens the philosopher with death if he does not speak. The emperor, however, has secretly arranged to have him executed if he *does* speak, but rescued if he remains silent. The literary form of this section is the *martyrology*, even though the narrative does not conclude with the death of Secundus. Secundus is depicted as a person who accepts death willingly rather than compromise his principles. Among the closer literary parallels to this section are the so-called acts of the pagan martyrs,[10] and the generically related acts of the Christian martyrs.[11] Closely related are stories of persecution and vindication of innocent people in Jewish literature.[12]

The third section consists of a scene before Hadrian which centers in a diatribe written for the benefit of Hadrian by Secundus. The purpose of this section is to prepare Hadrian for instruction by showing how weak and foolish humans are when compared with animals, and to attack the vanity and pride which Hadrian has even though he is hardly a match for the great men of antiquity. The diatribe is a classroom style which consists of a dialogical speech in which a teacher (usually a philosopher) addresses a student. In this speech Secundus uses some of the characteristic stylistic features of the diatribe such as rhetorical questions, hypothetical objections, false conclusions, and examples.

The fourth part consists of a question-and-answer dialogue in which Secundus submits written answers to a list of twenty questions formulated by Hadrian. This "dialogue" is also a popular literary form with parallels in Greco-Roman literature.[13] Though some scholars have proposed that this section circulated independently, all the evidence suggests that it was originally composed by the unknown author for inclusion at this particular point in the narrative.[14] This particular "dialogue" consists of twenty independent sets of questions and answers with no overall logical arrangement. The questions, all involving definitions and all

---

[10] Perry, *Secundus* 6–7; H. A. Musurillo, *The Acts of the Pagan Martyrs: Acta Alexandrinorum* (Oxford: Clarendon Press, 1954). A critical edition of the Greek texts is now available: Herbert Musurillo, *Acta Alexandrinorum* (Leipzig: B. G. Teubner, 1961).

[11] H. A. Musurillo, *The Acts of the Christian Martyrs* (Oxford: Clarendon Press, 1972).

[12] George W. E. Nickelsburg, "The Genre and Function of the Markan Passion Narrative," *HTR*, 73 (1980) 153–84. Examples include Gen 37–41; Esther; Dan. 3 and 6; Susanna; Wisdom of Sol 2–5; 2 Macc 7.

[13] The most extensive discussion of this form in by Lloyd W. Daley, *The Altercatio Hadriani Augusti et Epicteti Philosophi and the Question-and-Answer Dialogue*, Illinois Studies in Language and Literature, Vol. 24, No. 1 (Urbana: University of Illinois Press, 1939).

[14] Daly, *Altercatio* 46–48; Perry, *Secundus* vii–viii.

introduced with the interrogative phrase "what is" (Greek: *ti esti;* Latin: *qui est*), conform to one of the three distinctive types of Pythagorean *akousmata* ("oral teachings") formulated as questions and answers, i.e., (1) definitions *(ti esti)* (2) superlatives *(ti malista),* (3) duties and obligations *(ti prakteon).*[15] The content of the twenty sets of questions and answers in the *Life of Secundus,* however, have no particular relationship to Pythagoreanism or any of the other major philosophical traditions of antiquity. They are without exception repartees which function more to underscore the wisdom of Secundus than to provide an elementary philosophical catechism for popular consumption. If the answers were formulated as questions and the questions as answers, the literary form would become that of the *riddle.* As they stand, however, the answers are striking in that they are not the *single* best answers (appropriate in a philosophical context), but rather each "answer" consists of from seven (No. 2) to twenty-one (No. 10) "answers" to each question, averaging eleven answers per question. The fact that the questions (posed by Hadrian) are paired with answers (formulated by Secundus) indicates that we are dealing with *chreiai,* a Greek rhetorical form often translated "anecdotes" or "aphorisms."

The closest literary parallel to part four is the *Altercatio Hadriani Augusti et Epicteti Philosophi* ("Dialogue between the Emperor Hadrian and Epictetus the Philosopher"), an anonymous treatise composed in the second or third cent. A.D., and containing seventy-three questions posed by Hadrian and answered by the Stoic philosopher Epictetus.[16] These answers too are clever and witty responses altogether devoid of philosophical content. Unlike the question-and-answer dialogue in the *Life of Secundus* most of the seventy-three questions are paired with single answers (exceptions: Nos. 24, 29, 32, 35, 37, 38, 52, 59, 67). In his *Banquet of the Seven Sages,* Plutarch includes nine written questions sent to Thales by Niloxenus the emissary of Amasis, king of Egypt (153A-D).[17] The first question is "What is the oldest thing?" The answer of Thales is "God, for he has no beginning." Other question-and-answer "dialogues" which are similar to the fourth section of the *Life of Secundus* are the *Questions and Answers in Genesis and Exodus* of Philo of Alexandria (mentioned in Eusebius *Hist. eccl.* 2.18.1, and extant only in Armenian), and Plutarch's *Table Talks,* which consist of short dialogues

---

[15] Iamblichus *Vita Pythagorica* 82–86; Walter Burkert, *Lore and Science in Ancient Pythagoreanism,* trans. E. L. Minar, Jr. (Cambridge: Harvard University Press, 1972) 166–92, esp. 167–68.

[16] Walther Suchier, *Die "Altercatio Hadriani Augusti et Epicteti Philosophi" nebst einigen verwandten Texten Herausgeben,* Illinois Studies in Language and Literature, Vol. 24, No. 2 (Urbana: University of Illinois Press, 1939).

[17] David E. Aune, "Septem Sapientium Convivium (Moralia 146B–164D)," *Plutarch's Ethical Writings and Early Christian Literature,* ed. H. D. Betz (Leiden: Brill, 1978), 51–105.

each of which is a discussion aimed at finding a solution for a particular problem, often phrased as a question, stated at the outset. Another related type of literature is exemplified by the so-called *Certamen Homeri et Hesiodi* ("Contest of Homer and Hesiod), one of the late Homerica, in which the famous bards engage in a wisdom contest by posing different questions to each other (315–21), none of which are logically related.

B. *Translation: Life of Secundus the Philosopher*

I. Secundus' Fateful Reunion with His Mother

Secundus was a philosopher. The entire time that he pursued the philosophic life, he practiced silence, following the Pythagorean life style.[a] The reason for his silence is revealed in the following story. When very young he was sent away for an education by his parents, and while at school his father passed away.[b] He had heard the saying "Every woman has loose morals; the virtuous woman has just escaped notice." Therefore when he had grown to maturity he returned to his home town presenting himself as a practising Cynic. He carried around a stick and a leather pouch and cultivated long hair and a beard. He rented a room in the home in which he had grown up, unrecognized by any of the servants or even by his own mother. He wanted to test the truth of that saying about women. He summoned one of the maids and offered to pay her six gold pieces to arrange a liaison, pretending that he was smitten with her mistress, his own mother. The maid took the money and was able to convince her mistress, offering her fifty gold pieces. The mistress agreed with the maid and responded: "In the evening I will arrange for him to slip in secretly and I will go to bed with him."[c] When the philosopher had made these arrangements through the maid, he sent ahead the

---

[a] This sentence contains a striking antithesis, for how (the author implies) could a philosopher pursue his vocation (necessarily involng what he said as well as how he lived) while maintaining complete and permanent silence? A five-year period of probationary silence (probably connected with keeping Pythagorean views secret) was required as a prerequisite for membership (Diogenes Laertius *Lives of Philosophers* 8.10; Iamblichus, *Life of Pythagoras* 40–41). Yet Pythagoreans may have practiced silence for extended periods of time after becoming full members. Pythagorean silence was proverbial from the fourth cent. B.C. on (Isocrates *Oration* 11.29). Another Pythagorean, Apollonius of Tyana, reportedly maintained five years of silence (Philostratus *Life of Apollonius* 1.14), though these were apparently not probationary years.

[b] Unlike most Greco-Roman biographies, the birth and forebears of Secundus are not mentioned and his education is barely referred to. These constitute similarities to the Gospels, since in Mark nothing is mentioned of Jesus' origins, while in Matthew and Luke (doubtless influenced by biographical conventions) birth stories and genealogies are included, though Luke alone relates a story from Jesus' youth.

[c] One reflection of the popular literary style of *Secundus* is the preference for direct discourse (e.g., He said, "I will!") rather than indirect discourse (e.g., He said that he would). This preference for direct discourse even characterizes Luke-Acts, one of the more literary authors of the NT.

fixings for dinner. When they finished eating and were heading for bed, she was expecting to have sexual intercourse with him. But he, embracing her as his own mother and staring at the breasts where he once nursed, fell asleep til early next morning. About dawn Secundus got up intending to leave. But she tried to prevent him saying, "Did you do this in order to condemn me?" But he replied, "No, my dear mother,[d] it is just that it is not right to defile the very place from which I emerged. By no means!"[e] She then asked him who he was.[f] He replied to her, "I am Secundus, your son." She condemned herself and unable to endure the shame, hanged herself. Secundus, realizing that his mother had died because of his tongue,[g] he made a decision not to speak the rest of his life. And he maintained silence until death.

II. Hadrian Tests Secundus

At about that time[h] the emperor Hadrian, present in Athens, learned about Secundus (for nothing worthwhile escaped his notice) and commanded his presence. When Secundus arrived, Hadrian wanted to determine if he were truly committed to his vow of silence. The emperor rose first and greeted him.[i] Secundus, however, maintained his accustomed silence. Hadrian then said, "Speak, philosopher, that we might learn about you, for it is impossible to discover your inner wisdom while you maintain silence. But Secundus continued to be silent. Then Hadrian said to him, "Secundus, before I came it was appropriate for you to maintain silence for you had no hearer more esteemed than yourself or no one able to understand your words. But now I am here and I am

---

[d] The expression *kyria meter*, "my dear mother," is a respectful form of address which is difficult to translate into idiomatic English; expressions like "madam mother," or "lady mother" seem too stilted.

[e] The phrase *me genoito*, "by no means" is a familiar formula of objection found fourteen times in Paul's letters (e.g., Rom 3:4, 6, 31) and often associated with the diatribe; cf. Stanley K. Stowers, *The Diatribe and Paul's Letter to the Romans* (Chico: Scholars Press, 1981), 135–36.

[f] This is an example of indirect discourse introduced by an optative following the past tense of a verb of asking or inquiring.

[g] The negative effects of the tongue constitute one of the focal concerns of James (1:26; 3:5–12). The topos of talkativeness was common in Greco-Roman popular morality; cf. William A. Beardslee, "De Garrulitate (Moralia 502B–515A)," *Plutarch's Ethical Writings and Early Christian Literature*, ed. H. D. Betz (Leiden: Brill, 1978), 264–288.

[h] The phrase "at about this time" *(kata de ton kairon ekeinon)*, is a temporal clause linking the story just told with the one immediately following, giving the impression that the second follows the first chronologically. The Gospels contain about two dozen such temporal formulas used to introduce new pericopes and to place them in apparent chronological order with the preceding pericopes. These formulas are all listed and discussed by K. L. Schmidt, *Der Rahmen der Geschichte Jesu* (Darmstadt: Wissenschaftliche Buchgesellschaft, 1964; originally published in 1919), 319 (index).

[i] By this act, which technically violated imperial protocol, Hadrian shows great respect for a philosopher who puts his beliefs into practice.

worthy. Speak out, present your address advocating virtue. But Secundus was neither awed by nor afraid of the Emperor. Hadrian was displeased and he told a certain tribune, "Compel the philosopher to address us." The tribune was realistic and said, "It may be possible to persuade lions and leopards and other wild animals to speak with a human voice, but not a stubborn philosopher." Then he summoned a Greek guard and said, "I do not want anyone who refuses to speak to the Emperor Hadrian to live. Lead him away and punish him." But Hadrian summoned the bodyguard and told him confidentially, "When you lead the philosopher away, chat with him along the way and encourage him to speak. If you can persuade him to answer you, behead him, but if he fails to answer lead him back here again unharmed." Secundus, still maintaining his silence, was then led away.[j] The guard in charge of him led him down to the Piraeus, for that was the location where people were customarily punished. And he said to him, "O Secundus, why will you die just for keeping silence? Speak and you will live. Grant life to yourself through speech. For the swan sings toward the end of its life and as many other birds make sounds with the voice given to them. No living creature is without sound. Change your mind therefore, for the additional time gained will prove sufficient for your slience." With such arguments as these he advised and enticed Secundus. But Secundus, disregarding his life, waited death silently, unmoved by these arguments. The guard, leading the man out to the customary place, said: "Secundus, stretch out your neck for the sword." Secundus stretched out his neck, bidding farewell to life in silence. The guard showed him the unsheathed sword saying, "O Secundus, buy off death with your voice!" But Secundus said nothing. The guard, taking him along, returned to Hadrian and said, "Lord Caesar, I bring Secundus back to you in the same state that you turned him over to me, maintaining silence unto death." Hadrian, amazed at the philosopher's self-control,[k] stood up and said, "Secundus, you have imposed the maintenance of silence upon yourself as a law, and I was unable to break your law. Take this writing-tablet, write on it and converse with me using your hand." Secundus took the tablet and wrote the following, "I, O Hadrian, was not afraid of you because of the threat of death. For killing me is the only thing in your power. For you are now the

---

[j] There is a superficial parallel between the silence of Secundus during his hearing before Hadrian and the silence of Jesus before the Jewish high priest (Mark 14:61; cf. Matt 26:63), Pilate (Mark 15:5; cf. Matt 27:14; John 19:8) and Herod (Luke 23:9). Yet in the trial of Jesus as presented in the Synoptic Gospels, references to the silence of Jesus is momentary, except for his silence before Herod (Luke 23:9). The silence of Jesus at his trial was linked in 1 Pet 2:22–23 with Isa 53:7 understood as messianic prophecy. In these various scenes, the silence of Jesus suggests that he is fully in command of the situation.

[k] Pythagoras was remembered as being silent and secretive, unemotional and practising strict self-control.

temporary ruler. You have authority neither over my voice or over what I have to say." Upon reading this, Hadrian responded, "You defend yourself well, but now give me your views on a number of other matters. I will put twenty questions to you.[1] The first of them is this: What is the cosmos?"

III. Secundus' Diatribe to Hadrian

Secundus again wrote in reply. "The cosmos, O Hadrian, is the composite of heaven and earth and everything in them,[m] which I will discuss shortly if you prove attentive to what is being said. For you are a human being, O Hadrian, as we all are, participants in every kind of suffering, we are the residue of corruption. The life of irrational animals is the same. Some are covered with scales, some with hair, some have defects, some are brightly adorned; they are all covered and protected by what was given them by nature. But you, O Hadrian, happen to be filled with apprehension. You, with a brief lifespan and subject to many sufferings, anticipate being wounded and pulled to pieces, being roasted by the sun and frozen by the north wind. Your laughter is a prelude to sorrow turning into tears. Is it the necessity of fate or divine necessity which determines our lives? We do not know where necessity comes from, which is passing by us today, and we do not know what tomorrow will bring.[n] Therefore do not disregard what I am saying, O Hadrian. Do not claim that you alone have traveled around the *kosmos*,[o] for it is the sun, moon and stars which have traveled through the *kosmos*. Neither consider yourself to be handsome, important, wealthy and the ruler of the inhabited world. Do you not know that as a human being you have been born to be a plaything of life controlled by Fortune and fate, sometimes high, at other times lower than Hades? Are you unable to learn about life, O Hadrian, from the many available examples? How rich was the king of the Lydians with his golden obols? Agamemnon, king of the Danaans was a great commander. Alexander king of the Macedonians

---

[1]According to the *Historia Augusta, Hadrian* 20.2, when at the Museum in Alexandria Hadrian asked many questions of the faculty there and was able to answer them himself. He also had public conversations with many artists and scholars, and among his favorite philosophers were Epictetus and Heliodorus (*Historia Augusta, Hadrian* 16.8–10).

[m]The view that the *kosmos* consists of heaven and earth and everything in them is typically Stoic, though this notion was the common possession of late Hellenistic philosophy; cf. H. von Arnim, *Stoicorum Veterum Fragmenta* (Stuttgart: Teubner, 1964), II, 527 (Chrysippus), 528 (Arius Didymus, an eclectic), 529 (Cleomedes); cf. Acts 17:24.

[n]The subject here is *anagke*, or "necessity," which is described in mysterious terms reminiscent of John 3:8 in which the wind (Greek: *pneuma*) is used as a metaphor for the divine Spirit (Greek: *pneuma*); in neither case do we know whence it comes or whither it goes.

[o]The author uses the word *kosmos* here in two senses, the first means "earth" (around which Hadrian has traveled extensively), and "universe" (around which only the heavenly bodies have traveled).

was daring and courageous. Herakles was bold; the Cyclops was wild; Odysseus was clever; Achilles was handsome. If Fortune deprived these men of their distinguishing characteristics, how much more will she do the same to you?ᵖ You are not handsome like Achilles, or clever like Odysseus, or wild like the Cyclops, or bold like Herakles, or courageous and daring like Alexander or a commander like Agamemnon, nor rich like Gyges the king of the Lydians.ᵠ I have written this for you, O Hadrian, by way of introduction. Let us now go on to other matters just as you requested.

IV. Twenty Questions-and-Answers

1. What is the Cosmos?

An incomprehensible mass,ʳ a perceptible structure, a discontinuous height, a self-generated plan, a shape with many facets, an eternal composition, a sustaining ether,ˢ a fixed wheel, the light of the sun, day, star, darkness, night, earth, air, water.

2. What is the Ocean?

An embracer of the cosmos, a wreathed boundary, a saline circumference, an Atlantic link, an encircler of nature, a solar beacon, a restrainer of the inhabited world.

3. What is God?

A self-generating good, a manifold image, a discontinuous height, a shape with many facets,ᵗ a problem difficult to comprehend, an immortal intellect, an omnipresent spirit, a sleepless eye, a force with many names, an omnipotent light.

4. What is Day?

An arena of misery, a twelve-hour race, a daily beginning, a reminder of life, an extension of the afternoon, vital interaction, an eternal number, a reflection of nature, a recurring memory.

ᵖThis sentence presents an *a fortiore* argument, usually introduced (as here) with a conditional clause with the phrase "how much more" introducing the apodasis (e.g. Matt 6:30; 7:11; 10:25; Luke 11:13; 12:28; Rom 5:10, 15, 17; 2 Cor 3:9, 11; Ignatius *Ephesians* 5:1, 2; 16:2).

ᵠThe author lists these famous people in reverse or chiastic order, a popular rhetorical technique not formally treated in ancient rhetorical handbooks.

ʳThough this translation cannot always reproduce it, the form of each answer set off by commas consists of two words, an adjective and a noun. Many of these words are compounds and occur very rarely.

ˢThe term "ether" (introduced into cosmology by Aristotle), was regarded as a fifth element (after earth, air, fire, and water), and is the stuff which permeates the heavens and causes the movement of heavenly bodies.

ᵗThis answer and the next are verbally identical with two answers in the first set, suggesting the identity between the Cosmos and God.

5. What is the Sun?

A heavenly eye, a competitor of night, an ethereal sphere, a cosmic correction, an undefiled flame, a continuous light, a gratuitous lamp, a heavenly traveler, an adornment of the day.

6. What is the Moon?

The purple hue of heaven, a nocturnal consolation, a night watch for sailors, a consolation for travelers, a successor of the sun, an enemy of the wicked, a sign of festivals, a repetition of months.

7. What is the Earth?

The foundation of the heavens, the center of the Cosmos, a spectacle without foundation, a floating root, an incomprehensible mass, the school house of life, a divinely created whole, a night watch of the moon, an incomprehensible spectacle, nurse of the rain showers, the protection and mother of produce, the cover of Hades, a place with many regions, the origin and place of reception of all things.

8. What is a Human Being?

Incarnate intellect, a vessel containing spirit, a receptacle of perception, a soul exhausted by toil, a temporary habitation, a passing apparition in time, an organism with bones, a spy upon life, a plaything of Fortune, a transient benefit, an expenditure of life, a fugitive from living, a rebel from the light, demanded by earth, an eternal corpse.

9. What is Beauty?

A painting of nature, a self-formed good, temporary good luck, a transient property, the ruin of a religious man, incarnate luck, a retinue of pleasures, a fading flower, an uncorrupted spell, the desire of people.

10. What is a Woman?

The desire of a man, a wild beast at home, the anxiety with which you arise, interwoven sexual desire, a lioness with whom you sleep, a serpent wearing clothes, a fight freely chosen, self-indulgence with whom you sleep, a daily penalty, a storm in the house, an obstacle to freedom from care, the ruin of the intemperate man, training ground for adulterers, a life of captivity, an expensive war, a worthless creature, a sufficient burden, a storm with nine winds, a poison snake, a service which produces people, a necessary evil.

11. What is a Friend?

A desirable name, a person unseen, a rare commodity, an encouragment in difficulty, a refuge from misfortune, support in distress, an observer of life, a person inaccessible, a substantial treasure, inaccessible good fortune.

12. What is a Farmer?

A servant of crops, an arbitrator of rain, accustomed to solitude, a landlubber merchant, a competitor with the forest, a facilitator of nutrition, a cultivator of fields, a physician of the earth, a planter of trees, an instructor of hills, the custom of hard work.

13. What is a Gladiator?

Death for sale, an exhibitor's sacrifice, a trained fate, a sanguineous art, a misstep of Fortune, a quick death, a trumpeted fate, an imminent death, an awful victory.

14. What is a Boat?

A sea-tossed object, a foundationless home, a well-crafted tomb, a wooden cubicle, a journey by wind, a flying prison, a confined fate, a plaything of the wind, sailing death, a wooden bird, a sea steed, an open cage, uncertain safety, the prospect of death, a traveler on the waves.

15. What is a Sailor?

A traveler by wave, a marine poster, a tracker of waves, a fellow traveler with the winds, a stranger to the inhabited world, a deserter of land, an adversary of the storm, a gladiator of the sea, uncertain of safety, a neighbor of death, one who loves the sea.

16. What is Wealth?

A golden burden, a servant of pleasure, a hopeful fear, thoughtless enjoyment, having envy as a roommate, a daily worry, an unstable condition, a precious misfortune, a treacherous condition, an insatiable desire, a many-faceted misfortune, a long fall, a monetary password, temporary good luck.

17. What is Poverty?

A despised blessing, the mother of health, an obstacle to pleasure, a carefree lifestyle, a possesion hard to lose, a teacher of resourcefulness, a discoverer of wisdom, an unenviable situation, a possession no one bothers, an untaxed commodity, an unwelcome advantage, an estate immune to swindlers, disguised good luck, good fortune without worry.

18. What is Old Age?

An evil honestly acquired, a living death, a healthy disease, an expected fate, a long-standing joke, the slackening of intelligence, a living corpse, a stranger to Aphrodite[u], the expectation of death, a moving cadaver.

---

[u] Here Aphrodite is the personification of sexual love.

19. What is Sleep?
Rest from labor, the success of physicians, the freedom of those confined, wisdom for the wakeful, the prayer of the sick, an image of death, the desire of the distressed, rest from every breath, the pursuit of the rich, a daily concern.

20. What is Death?
Eternal sleep, the dissolution of the body, the desire of the distressed, the desertion of the spirit, the fear of the rich, the desire of the poor, the slackening of the limbs, the flight from, and loss of, life, the father of sleep, an appointment truly prearranged, the end of all.

When Hardian had read this and had learned the reason why Secundus pursued the philosophic life in silence, he ordered hs books placed in the sacred library under "Secundus the Philosopher."

D. Relation to Early Christian Literature

The Gospels focus on the life of Jesus, or at least aspects of his life, emphasizing sayings and actions. While it might seem very natural to compare the Gospels with the biographical literature of antiquity, the prevailing opinion among most New Testament scholars has been that whatever the Gospels are, they are certainly *not* biographies.[18] Recent scholarship has been less willing to accept that view, and many studies have appeared which have attempted to compare the Gospels with Greco-Roman biography.[19]

1. Are the Gospels Unique?

While it is true that the Gospels are *unique* in certain respects, it is also true that many other ancient compositions which scholars have unhesitatingly categorized as "biography" are also "unique" (e.g. Lu-

---

[18] For a competent survey of research in this question, see Robert Guelich, "The Gospel Genre," *Das Evangelium und die Evangelien* (Tübingen: Mohr, 1983), pp. 183–219. In the same volume the classicist Albrecht Dihle argues for the uniqueness of the Gospels in his article "Die Evangelien und die griechische Biographie," pp. 383–411. See also Aune, *The New Testament in Its Literary Environment* 17–36, 46–76.

[19] For example, see C. H. Talbert, *What is a Gospel?*; idem, *Literary Patterns, Theological Themes, and the Genre of Luke-Acts* (Missoula: Scholars Press, 1974); Martin Hengel, *Acts and the History of Earliest Christianity* (Philadelphia: Fortress, 1979) 3–34; David L. Barr and Judith L. Wentling, "The Conventions of Classical Biography and the Genre of Luke-Acts: A Preliminary Study," *Luke-Acts: New Perspectives from the Society of Biblical Literature Seminar*, ed. C. H. Talbert (New York: Crossroad, 1984) 63–88; Philip L. Shuler, *A Genre for the Gospels: The Biographical Character of Matthew* (Philadelphia: Fortress, 1982); Vernon K. Robbins, *Jesus the Teacher: A Socio-Rhetorical Interpretation of Mark* (Philadelphia: Fortress, 1984).

cian's *Demonax*, Tacitus' *Agricola*, Philostratus' *Life of Apollonius*). This suggests that neither the category of "the unique" or the quality of "uniqueness" tells us very much about an ancient composition. Rather, it is important to know both the ways in which the Gospels are similar to and differ from ancient biographical literature.

The unique character of the Gospels lies primarily in the uniqueness of their *content*, determined by their subject: Jesus of Nazareth, who taught that the Kingdom of God was provisionally present in both his teachings and miracles, and who had been executed as a revolutionary but had conquered death through resurrection. The Gospels, each of which elaborated on these connected themes in various ways, were read by early Christians within the context of a belief that Jesus was the Messiah of Jewish expectation and further that he was the pre-existent Son of God who had been exalted to the right hand of God until he would return in power and glory at the climax of history to judge the living and the dead. No Greco-Roman biography depicts a life even remotely comparable to that of Jesus.

Yet in both *form* and *function*, the Gospels are fully comparable to Greco-Roman biography. In *form*, the Gospels (particularly Mark and John) focus on the public career of Jesus. The authors of Matthew and Luke, who have more consciously literary concerns than Mark, follow accepted biographical practice by prefacing the career of Jesus with accounts of his birth and genealogy. Jesus himself is presented in the appropriate stereotypes associated with the titles Messiah and Prophet. The *function* of the Gospels was the legitimation of the present beliefs and practices of Christians by appealing to the paradigmatic role of the founder, just as the cultural values of the Hellenistic world were exemplified by the subjects of Greco-Roman biographies. The Gospels, then, represent an adaptation of Greco-Roman biographical conventions used to convey a life of unique religious significance for Christians.

2. The Emphasis on Martyrdom

The Gospel of Mark has been aptly described as a passion story with an extended introduction. About 20% of Mark focuses on the arrest, trial, execution and resurrection of Jesus. This emphasis is partly the consequence of the theological significance of Jesus' death in early Christianity. However, that cannot fully account for such am emphasis. In Mark the atoning significance of Jesus' death is mentioned just once (10:45), in a passage taken over by Matthew (20:28). In Luke-Acts, which contains no indication that Jesus' death is atoning, Jesus dies as a prophet-martyr. Most Greco-Roman biographies (with some major exceptions) are not as interested in the deaths of their subjects as the Gospels are in the death of Jesus. Yet in many ancient cultures the origin of biography was closely associated with epitaphs and eulogies. In the late Hellenistic and early Roman periods there was a marked increase in the emphasis on death, particularly violent death and marytrdom, in biographical literature. This is reflected in the many anonymous (and largely fictional) lives of Greek poets,[20] in the late lives of philosophers by Dionysius Laertius (ca. third century A.D.), and in the thumbnail sketches of Israelite prophets in the anonymous *Lives of the Prophets* (ca. first century A.D.). Plutarch's life of *Cato the Younger* focuses on his exemplary death. Short lives emphasizing the demise of famous men (a kind of martyr literature), a subgenre of biography, were fashionable at the end of the first century A.D. Gaius Fannius wrote about the deaths of famous men executed under Nero (Pliny *Letters* 5.5.1–3), and Titinius Capito (who wrote *Exitus illustrium virorum*, "Departure of Famous Men") specialized in death scenes. The same fashion was followed by Tacitus (cf. his narratives of the final days of Seneca (*Annals* 15.60–64), and of Thrasea and Soramus (*Annals* 16.21–35). According to an ancient Greek conception, a person's life could be evaluated only when completed by death (Herodotus 1.30–32). One of the forerunners of biography was the epic tradition celebrating the valiant deeds of the hero whose death had rescued him from oblivion and made him memorable, thereby giving him "individuality."[21] The Greeks therefore placed a high value on the "good" death of the hero (Iliad 9.410–16).[22] The exemplary death of Socrates had a powerful impact on ancient martyr literature, both Greco-Roman and Christian.[23] Among pagans and Christians, calmness and courage in the face of death was celebrated (cf. Mark 14:32–42, 53–65; 15:2–5 and par.; John 18:29–38; 19:8–15), particularly as a prelude to voluntary suicide rather than public execution (Pliny *Letters* 3.16; Tacitus *Annals* 11.3). The focus on the death of Jesus which characterizes all of the Gospels, then, is a theme characteristic of a development in Greco-Roman biography of the first century A.D.

3. The Inclusive Character of the Gospels

The Gospels, like Greco-Roman biography generally, are examples of an inclusive literary form into which a variety of shorter literary forms may be inserted. In our discussion above, we saw that the *Life of*

[20] Mary R. Lefkowitz, *The Lives of the Greek Poets* (Baltimore: Johns Hopkins, 1981).

[21] J.-P. Vernant, "Death with Two Faces," *Mortality and Immortality: The Anthropology and Archaeology of Death*, ed. S. C. Humphreys and H. King (London: Academic Press, 1981) 285–91.

[22] Jasper Griffin, *Homer on Life and Death* (Oxford: The Clarendon Press, 1980); Emily Vermeule, *Aspects of Death in Early Greek Art and Poetry* (Berkeley: University of California Press, 1979) 83–117; Sally Humphreys, "Death and Time," *The Family, Women and Death: Comparative Studies* (London: Routledge & Kegan Paul, 1983) 144–164.

[23] Klaus Döring, *Exemplum Socratis: Studien zur Sokratesnachwirkung in der kynisch-stoischen Popularphilosophie der frühen Kaiserzeit und im frühen Christentum*, Hermes Einzelschriften, Heft 42 (Wiesbaden: Franz Steiner, 1979).

Secundus serves as a literary framework for a novella, a martyrology, a diatribe and a question-and-answer dialogue constructed of many individual *chreiai* (i.e., anecdotes) resembling expanded *gnomai* (i.e., maxims). The Gospels include a great variety of literary forms, some of which are simple and others relatively complex.

Among the shorter, simpler forms are those which have been identified using the methodology of form criticism. Though this method often assumes that the forms identified once circulated *orally*, that assumption is difficult to prove. The Synoptic Gospels contain five main categories of such forms: (1) about three dozen *chreiai* or anecdotes, often called pronouncement stories (e.g., Mark 2:15–17; 3:22–27; 10:17–22), (2) about sixty-five parables (e.g. Mark 4:1–9, 26–29, 30–32), (3) twenty-nine miracles stories in all four Gospels (e.g., Mark 1:21–28, 29–31; 5:1–20; John 2:1–11), (4) many *stories about Jesus* (e.g., the baptism, Mark 1:9–11; the temptation (Mark 1:12–13; Matt 4:1–11; Luke 4:1–13), and (5) a variety of *sayings of Jesus* (Mark 1:15; 3:4; 7;15). While anecdotes were used for the purpose of conveying the virtues of the subject in Greco-Roman biographies, it is clear that they have an entirely different purpose in the Gospels. In the Gospels most of the shorter literary forms contribute to identifying Jesus in terms of the stereotypical role associated with the titles Messiah and Son of God (cf. Mark 1:1).

The longer and more complex the literary unit identified in the Gospels, the more likely it is that it existed in literary or written forms before inclusion into one of the Gospels. The most extensive such literary form is the Passion Narrative (Mark 14–16 and parallels), widely thought to have existed prior to its inclusion in Mark. The extensive nature of the Passion Narrative, with its martyrological features, has resulted in an emphasis on the trial and execution of Jesus which, in spite of its unique significance to Christians, has parallels in the first-century Greco-Roman biography as discussed above. The Synoptic Gospels also contain sermons, some of which (like the Sermon on the Mount in Matt 5–7) probably existed prior to the inclusion in the Gospels, even though they were constructed out of shorter sayings of Jesus. The Gospel of John differs to a considerable extent from the Synoptic Gospels in both content and structure. While John does contain seven miracle stories, the most distinctive feature of the Fourth Gospel is the Johannine discourses and dialogues. These exhibit great variety and have yet to be analyzed adequately. The discourses included (1) monologues (5:19–47; 12:20–36), (2) monologues framed by dialogue (16:16–30), (3) dramatic dialogues (4:7–27; 6:25–59), and (4) short controversy dialogues (7:14–24; 8:12–20).

4. The Historical Intentions of the Evangelists

History and biography were closely related types of writing in Greco-Roman antiquity which ancient men of letters tried to keep separate

(Polybius 10.21.5–8; Plutarch *Alexander* 1.1–3; *Niceas* 1.5; Cornelius Nepos *Pelopidas* 1.1). Anecdotes, maxims and reminiscences, for example, were thought appropriate for inclusion in biographies but not in histories. Ideally, history ought to be truthful, useful and entertaining (Lucian *How to Write History* 9). The material for biography was often gotten from historical works (this, for example, was the usual procedure of Plutarch), but the accent was placed upon the subjects as paradigms of virtue and (less frequently) vice. Thus while biography tended to emphasize ecomium, or the one-sided praise of the subject, it was still firmly rooted in historical fact rather than literary fiction. Thus while the Evangelists clearly had an important theological agenda, the very fact that they chose to adapt Greco-Roman biographical conventions to tell the story of Jesus indicates that they were centrally concerned to communicate what they thought really happened.

E. Annotated Bibliography

The classical discussion of Greco-Roman biography is Friedrich Leo's *Griechisch-römische Biographie nach ihrer litterarischen Form* (Leipzig: Teubner, 1901). Some of the more important studies since Leo include Duane Reed Stuart, *Epochs of Greek and Roman Biography* (Berkeley: University of California Press, 1928), Wolf Steidle, *Sueton und die antike Biographie* (Munich: Beck, 1951), Albrecht Dihle, *Studien zur griechischen Biographie* (Göttingen: Vandenhoeck & Ruprecht, 1956), and particularly recommended is Arnaldo Momigliano, *The Development of Greek Biography* (Cambridge: Harvard University Press, 1971).

The most important discussion of the anonymous biography of Secundus including texts and an extensive bibliography, is Ben Edwin Perry, *Secundus the Silent Philosopher*, APA Monographs, 22 (Ithaca: The American Philological Association and Cornell University Press, 1964). Also important is Lloyd W. Daly and Walter Suchier, *Altercatio Hadriani Augusti et Epicteti Philosophi*, Illinois Studies in Language and Literature, vol. 24, nos. 1–2 (Urbana: University of Illinois Press, 1939), 44–70.

For Greco-Roman biographies available in English translation, see Plutarch's *Lives* and Suetonius, *Lives of the Caesars*, completed about A.D. 120, contains biographies of twelve Roman emperors from Julius Caesar to Domitian. For a helpful guide to Suetonius, see Andrew Wallace-Hadrill, *Suetonius: The Scholar and His Caesars* (New Haven: Yale University Press, 1983). For a competent discussion of the anonymous biographies of Greek poets with translations (in the Appendices) of eight lives (Homer, Pindar, Aeschylus, Sophocles, Euripides, Aristophanes, Plato and Antimachus), see Mary R. Lefkowitz, *The Lives of the Greek Poets* (Baltimore: The Johns Hopkins University Press, 1981).

On Pythagoreanism, see particularly Walter Burkert, *Lore and Science in Ancient Pythagoreanism*, trans. E. L. Minar, Jr. (Cambridge; Harvard University Press, 1972). See also Peter Gorman, *Pythagoras: A Life* (London: Routledge & Kegan Paul, 1979); C. J. De Vogel, *Pythagoras and Early Pythagoreanism* (Assen, 1966); Holger Thesleff, *Introduction to the Pythagorean Writings of the Hellenistic Period* (Abo, 1961); *Idem, The Pythagorean Texts of the Hellenistic Period* (Abo, 1965).

For an extensive discussion of the relationship between Greco-Roman biographical literature and the Gospels, see David E. Aune, *The New Testament in its Literary Environment* (Philadelphia: Westminster, 1987), 17–76. Also important is Klaus Berger, "Hellenistische Gattungen im Neuen Testament," *Aufstieg und Niedergang der römischen Welt*, Part II, Vol. 25/2 (New York and Berlin: W. de Gruyter, 1984), 1231–43, "Biographie," contains a helpful synopsis of extant Greek and Latin biographies together with a discussion of the problems involved in regarding the canonical Gospels as biography.

On the form criticism of the Gospels the classical discussions are those of Martin Dibelius, *From Tradition to Gospel*, trans. B. L. Woolf (New York: Scribner's, n.d.), and Rudolf Bultmann, *The History of the Synoptic Tradition*, trans. J. Marsh (New York and Evanston: Harper & Row, 1963). Also helpful is Vincent Taylor, *The Formation of the Gospel Tradition* (London: Macmillan, 1953), who simplifies the form-critical categories of Dibelius and Bultmann. On *chreiai* see Ronald F. Hock and Edward N. O'Neill, *The Chreia in Ancient Rhetoric*, Volume I: *The Progymnasmata* (Atlanta: Scholars Press, 1986); John Dominic Crossan, *In Fragments: The Aphorisms of Jesus* (San Francisco: Harper & Row, 1983); Arland J. Hultgren, *Jesus and His Adversaries: The Form and Function of the Conflict Stories in the Synoptic Tradition* (Minneapolis: Augsburg, 1979).

CHAPTER 7
THE GREEK NOVEL

Ronald F. Hock
University of Southern California

I. Introduction

The words "novel" and "romance" (an alternative name for this genre) are clearly modern literary categories, but scholars also use them, fittingly enough, for a number of ancient Greek narratives of love, those entertaining and informative stories of love sorely tried and proved true. Five complete examples of this genre are extant: Achilles Tatius' *Clitophon and Leucippe,* Chariton's *Callirhoe,* Heliodorus' *Ethiopian Tale,* Longus' *Daphnis and Chloe,* and Xenophon's *Ephesian Tale.* In addition, other, largely Byzantine, sources provide summaries or titles of otherwise lost novels, and the sands of Egypt continue to supply papyrus fragments of still more. These latter discoveries—*Ninus and Semiramis, Metiochus and Parthenope,* and Lollianus' *Phoenician Tale,* to name the most important—are valuable additions for a variety of reasons, not the least of which is that they further underscore how widespread and popular this genre was in antiquity.

A. *History of Research*
Scholarship on the Greek novel—from Rohde's magisterial, if dated, *Der griechische Roman und seine Vorläufer* (1876, ³1914) to more recent general treatments, such as Perry's *The Ancient Romances* (1967), Reardon's *Courants littéraires grecs des IIe et IIIe siècles après J.-C.* (1971), and Hägg's *The Novel in Antiquity* (1983)—has concerned itself with two tasks. On the one hand, scholars have focused on the preliminary tasks of investigating the novels' dates, origins, types, and specialized problems and on producing texts, translations, commentaries, and related tools. On the other hand, they have sought to interpret the novels themselves, though largely in literary terms. The following survey of this scholarship will take up these two concerns in turn.

Scholarly opinion regarding the dates of the novels has changed dramatically during the past century, with some novels receiving dates much earlier than formerly and others later. The most dramatic change has involved the date of Chariton's novel. Rohde (*Roman*, 521–22) regarded this novel to be the latest of all and in fact assigned it to the fifth or sixth century A.D. But papyrus fragments of this novel from the second or third century have rendered Rohde's opinion untenable. Consequently, scholars today place Chariton much earlier, perhaps as early as the first century B.C. (so Papanikalaou, *Chariton-Studien*, 7–8), though most scholars favor the mid first century A.D. (see further Plepelits, *Chariton*, 5–6). Chariton's *Callirhoe* thereby becomes the earliest of the extant novels.

The dating of Heliodorus' *Ethiopian Tale* has also changed, though not as dramatically nor as convincingly. Rohde (*Roman*, 496) assigned this novel to the second half of the third century (so also Perry, *Romances*, 349 n. 13), but more recent discussion is tending toward the late fourth (so Reardon, *Courants*, 334 n. 57; cf. Sandy, *Heliodorus*, 1–5, and Bowie, "Novel," 696).

Accordingly, when these recent debates are all taken into consideration (on which see further Perry, *Romances*, 348–52; Reardon, *Courants*, 333–37; and Bowie, "Novel," 684), the following sequence and dating emerges:

Chariton, *Callirhoe* (mid first century A.D.)
Xenophon, *Ephesian Tale* (early or mid second century [cf. Gärtner, "Xenophon," 2086–87])
Achilles Tatius, *Clitophon and Leucippe* (mid to late second century [cf. Reardon, *Courants*, 334 n. 56])
Longus, *Daphnis and Chloe* (late second to early third century [cf. Hunter, *Study*, 3–15])
Heliodorus, *Ethiopian Tale* (late fourth century).

As this list makes clear, the second century is especially well represented, and the evidence of other novels only confirms this tendency. Thus, Iamblichus' *Babylonian Tale*, which Photius (*Bibl.* Cod. 94.10) has summarized, belongs to the late second century (cf. Hägg, *Novel*, 32); to the early second century belong *Araspes and Panthea*, known from Philostratus (*VS* 524) and attributed, perhaps falsely, to the sophist Demetrius of Miletus, and the *Phoenician Tale*, attributed, again perhaps falsely, to the sophist Lollianus of Ephesus (cf. Bowie, "Novel," 686). *Metiochus and Parthenope* probably also belongs to the early second century, though a first century dating is possible (cf. Bowie, "Novel," 684). Only the *Ninus* romance breaks the pattern, since its accepted dating is c. 100 B.C. (cf. Perry, *Romances*, 153). Accordingly, it is earlier than Chariton's *Callirhoe* and thus the earliest known example of the genre.

In addition to dating, scholars have been especially busy investigating the origins of the novel. Some scholars have sought the origin in solely literary terms, an approach associated particularly with Rohde. He regarded erotic poetry and travel narratives as the principal *Vorläufer* of the novel (see esp. *Roman*, 178–83). But similarities between the novels and other literary forms—epic, historiography, biography, drama, and comedy—have suggested to others a more complex literary pedigree for the novel (see further Hägg, *Novel*, 109–24).

Perry, however, reacted strongly to this literary approach in which a supposed biological analogy of one genre "developing" gradually out of another motivated the search for literary antecedents as well as an equally external idealist literary theory (see *Romances*, 3–43). Perry preferred to emphasize the role of the individual in producing the first novel. Hence his oft-quoted remark: "The first romance was deliberately planned and written by an individual author, its inventor. He conceived it on a Tuesday afternoon in July, or some other day or month of the year. It did not come into being by a process of development on the literary plane" (*Romances*, 175).

Instead of the literary plane Perry looked to the cultural context, and what was paramount here was his understanding of late Alexandrian society (like the modern period which also produced the novel) as an "open" society—big, stratified, and centrifugal (see *Romances*, 335 n. 15)—in which the novel, itself the least defined, most formless of genres, was thus the most genuine and characteristic expression of an open society, an open form, as it were, for an open society (cf. *Romances*, 29).

Perry's views have been influential, especially his claim that the novel was a particularly good "fit" for articulating late Hellenistic and early imperial experience. Indeed, scholars have extended his analysis through such notions as Reardon's "personal myth," which the novel represents, in contrast to the "political myth" of Greek tragedy and the "social myth" of New Comedy (cf. Reardon, "Novel," 292–94), or through more detailed descriptions of Hellenistic society and the particular circles involved with the first novels: scribes reading novels aloud to women or young people in the urban households of Asia Minor (so Hägg, *Novel*, 82–101).

Recently, however, Anderson has challenged Perry's views of the origin of the novel by arguing that the novel "is not a product of the Hellenistic World" (Anderson, *Fiction*, 19); rather, the novel began much, much earlier at Sumer with such romantic tales as *Dumuzi's*

Dream and *Enlil and Ninlil*. Thus what the first Greek novelist did on Perry's Tuesday afternoon in July was not so much invent the genre as retell an old story in a new cultural context (cf. *Fiction*, 1, 25–27).

Anderson's thesis is certain to provoke lively discussion, for even though he speaks of "proof" (cf. *Fiction*, 6), there are several questions and problems with it. Many of the parallels between the novels and their Ancient Near Eastern counterparts are not as close as Anderson's discussion assumes, and those that are might not require literary dependence to explain them. Nor does Anderson adequately explain how the novelists learned of these old stories and why they made use of them only in the late Hellenistic period. And, finally, the whole argument seems to serve an apologetic purpose: to excuse Greek writers for treating so unclassical a subject as young love by tracing the stories themselves back to non-Greek sources; consequently, the novelists are held responsible only for the skills and techniques they used in retelling these stories (cf. *Fiction*, 3, 19, 38). It is clear, however, that the century-long debate on the origins of the novel is far from resolved.

Another subject of scholarship on the novel has been classification, for not only do the many differences among the extant novels invite subclassification, but similarities with other writings raise questions of whether to classify them, too, in some way with the novels. The five extant novels differ in many ways that distinguish one from the others—for example, the length and complexity of Heliodorus, the pastoral setting of Longus, the first-person narrative of Achilles Tatius—but one difference in particular has led to assigning sub-types among these novels. Compared to the relatively simple narratives of Chariton and Xenophon, those of Achilles Tatius, Longus, and Heliodorus have a more artistic prose and contain numerous digressive episodes and descriptions—one thinks of, say, Achilles Tatius' discussion of the hippopotamus (4.2–5) or Longus' elaborate description of Dionysophanes' garden (4.2–4). These features suggest the influence of the literary trends of the early imperial movement known as the Second Sophistic. Accordingly, these novels are sometimes termed "sophistic" and the others "pre-sophistic" (cf. Perry, *Romances*, 108–9; Hägg, *Novel*, 34–35; and Anderson, *Fiction*, 53). One consequence of this distinction is the likelihood that the sophistic novels were intended for a more educated and so smaller audience than the earlier novels had been (cf. Hägg, *Novel*, 107–8).

The related question of classification concerns how many other narrative writings to include under at least a general category of novel. Consequently, the five novels are now termed "ideal romances," so that others can be classed as "comic romances:" Lucian's *Ass*, Apuleius' *Metamorphoses*, and Petronius' *Satyricon* (cf. Perry, *Romances*, 87–95).

Indeed, many narratives with romantic or travel themes are sometimes included with the novels proper: Antonius Diogenes' *Marvels* beyond Thule (cf. Hägg, Novel, 118–21), Dio Chrysostom's so-called Euboean discourse (=Orat. 7.1–81; cf. Jouan, "Thèmes"), the Menander-Glycera correspondence (=Alciphron, Ep. 4.18–19; cf. Anderson, Fiction, 39–40), Joseph and Aseneth (cf. West, "Joseph"), and such Christian writings as The Acts of Paul and Thecla (cf. Hägg, Novel, 154–62) and the canonical Acts (cf. Schierling and Schierling, "Influence"). But whether these writings are novels is less important than the fact that they all benefit from comparisons with the novel.

Finally, scholars have identified various introductory issues regarding individual novels. A mere sampling will indicate the range: whether Chariton's novel was originally named *Callirhoe* rather than *Chaereas and Callirhoe* (cf. Plepelits, Chariton, 28–29); whether Xenophon's novel, as we have it, is an epitome of a longer work (so Bürger, "Xenophon," but opposed by Hägg, "Ephesiaka"); whether Achilles Tatius wrote his novel as a parody (cf. Durham, "Parody"); whether Longus had a definite locale on Lesbos in mind for the setting of his story (cf. Green, "Longus"); and whether Heliodorus was later a Christian bishop, as later tradition claims (cf. Sandy, Heliodorus, 3–4).

When scholars move from these various introductory matters to the task of interpreting the novels themselves, they have largely asked literary questions and so have adopted literary methods. Especially noteworthy in this regard are the detailed and sophisticated analyses in Hägg's *Narrative Technique in Ancient Greek Romances* (1971). Hägg introduces concepts from modern literary criticism to analyze Chariton, Xenophon, and Achilles Tatius, and Reardon ("Chariton," 7–11) has shown the value of this literary approach by building on Hägg's analysis and statistics to identify the theme, structure, and narrative technique in Chariton. For example, Reardon insightfully distinguishes between the power of love, which is centered in Callirhoe, as the theme of the novel and Chaereas and his rivals for her love as giving the novel its structure. And Anderson (*Fiction*, 136–51) has perceptively analyzed the various novelists' storytelling techniques so that their individual skills and outlooks come sharply into focus. The overall consequence of these literary studies has been a much needed reevaluation of the novels. Thus whereas Rohde (*Roman*, 549) once dismissed Longus, for example, with the contemptuous epithet "sophist," Anderson (*Fiction*, 144) now credits him with having written a "classic." Only Xenophon has not benefitted from this reappraisal, as Anderson (*Fiction*, 144–48 and *passim*) never tires of pointing out.

This literary approach, as insightful as it has been, nevertheless given a narrow or restricted view of the novels, so that their interpretation has suffered from a neglect of other modes of analysis. For example, the use of modern literary critical concepts has been at the expense of ancient rhetorical categories, even though all recognize the influence of rhetoric on the "sophistic" novels but it is no less clear for the earlier ones. To be sure, Anderson (*Fiction*, 43–61) rightly sees the association of romance and rhetoric, but his use of rhetorical concepts is neither incisive nor sustained. Hunter (*Study*, 84–98) goes farther in relating Longus' style to the rhetorical theory of Hermogenes, but much remains to be done before Astylos' remark, that Eros makes great orators (Longus, 4.18.1), is fully appreciated for the novels as a whole.

Another analytic perspective, long neglected but beginning to emerge, is that of social history, as the social and economic dimensions of Xenophon's and Longus' novels have received some attention (so Scarcella, "Structures" and "Realtà"), though especially well done is Millar's analysis of Apuleius' related *Metamorphoses* (see Millar, "World;" cf. Winkler, "Lollianos"). Still, because of their length, detail, and coherence the novels are exceptionally important sources for reconstructing the social world of the early Roman empire in virtually all its aspects—from the experiences of urban aristocrats to those of brigands in the hills. Indeed, by reading the novels for their distinctive *mentalité*, the ways they made sense of their world, we will gain a much clearer notion of where they belong in early imperial society.

A final approach to interpreting the novels, the history of religions, has been largely abandoned. Kerényi (*Die griechisch-orientalische Roman-literatur in religionsgeschichtlicher Beleuchtung*, 1927) and Merkelbach (*Roman und Mysterium in der Antike*, 1962) had pushed a thoroughly religious interpretation in which the novels are viewed as little more than coded reworkings of religious myth—say, the myth of Isis in Xenophon's *Ephesian Tale* (Merkelbach, *Mysterium*, 91–113). They seem to have pushed too hard. This thesis has received little support. Gärtner ("Xenophon," 2074–80) has a detailed criticism of it with respect to Xenophon. More generally, Perry (*Romances*, 336 n. 17) dismissed the thesis, calling it "nonsense." Reardon (*Courants*, 318–19) is more reserved but no more favorable, a position echoed up to the present (Hägg, *Novel*, 101–4; Anderson, *Eros*, 107 n. 62; and Hunter, *Study*, 111 n. 69).

As a result scholars are increasingly loath to admit any religious intention on the part of the novelists, at least the best ones, preferring to emphasize the literary aim as primary. Thus Anderson (*Fiction*, 85) says: "The ablest authors are able to use religion as a servant of fiction." Longus is clearly one of the ablest and he, according to Anderson (*Fiction*, 136), only looks "with gentle amusement" at people who travel to Lesbos to worship the nymphs (cf. Longus, *praef.* 1). In contrast, Xenophon, about whom Anderson (*Fiction*, 147) finds it "surprisingly hard to say anything good," is supposedly not so detached but is "genuinely convinced that Habrocomes could have been saved by divine intervention from crucifixion" (*Fiction*, 81; cf. Xenophon, 4.2). More generally: "The other ideal novels embody art and (relative) lack of piety;

Xenophon genuine piety and lack of art" (Anderson, *Eros*, 63; cf. Perry, *Romances*, 31, 35, 45; Hägg, *Novel*, 26). But even if Xenophon's literary skills do not match those of the others, his piety is not the cause, and the others—Longus included—are not any less pious. The religious dimension in the novels clearly needs a new and more sympathetic analysis.

In sum, scholarship on the interpretation of the novels has made significant progress at the level of literary analysis. But the emphasis on literary skill, technique, and intention has left undone incisive, sophisticated, and fair investigations of the rhetorical, social, and religious dimensions of the novel. Carrying out these investigations will require an interdisciplinary effort.

B. Formal Features

The novel, ancient or modern, is hardly a genre with a rigid formal structure. In fact, the opposite is the case. Perry (*Romances*, 29) said: "Of all the recognized literary forms, the romance, or novel, is by nature the most unbounded and the least confined in the range of what it may include." Consequently, to term the Greek novel, formally speaking, a "narrative" is true enough but useful only in the most general sense. A little more precision is gained, if we, as the ancient rhetoricians did, distinguish various kinds of narrative—mythical, dramatic, and historical. The novel would be an example of the dramatic in that it is fabricated but not so imaginative as to be fabulous, as is the case with the myth or fable; and it is realistic but only in the sense that its actions could have happened, not that its actions actually happened, as is the case with history (cf. Aphthonius, *Progymn.* 2 [p. 2 Rabe], and Nicolaus, *Progymn.* 3 [pp. 12–13 Felten]; cf. Barwick, "Gliederung").

Still, any formal analysis of the novel, while granting its overall form as a dramatic narrative, must focus on the units that make up the whole, and at this level variety of forms is the rule. And perhaps pride of place should be given to the speech, for one way that Eros makes great orators (cf. Longus, 4.18.1) is suggested by the great number of speeches the principal characters deliver in the course of the novels. In fact, the novelists seem to manipulate their plots so as to give their characters as many opportunities as possible to give a speech. Speeches are frequent in Chariton's novel, with the theatre in Syracuse the site for many speeches (cf. 1.5.3–6.2; 3.4.3–18; 8.7.1–11). But Babylon is where the speech achieves its dramatic prominence. Dionysius and Mithridates appear before the Great King, Dionysius to charge Mithridates with adultery on the basis of a love letter Dionysius believed the other had forged in Chaereas' name, and Mithridates to defend himself. Chariton lavishes much attention on the preparation for the trial and includes Dionysius' speech verbatim (5.6.1–10). As well as that of Mithridates (5.7.1–7). Dionysius' letter is legitimate evidence for a charge of adultery (cf. Quintilian, 7.2.52), and his speech conforms to the pattern of speeches of accusation, with its introduction (Chariton, 5.6.1–4), statement of the case (5.6.5–8), proof (5.6.9), and conclusion (5.6.10). Mithridates' speech of defense is likewise narrated verbatim and according to form, but he gains his acquittal by demonstrating that he had not written the damning letter. He uses a familiar technique of conclusions (cf. Quintilian, 4.1.28) by calling (the not so) dead Chaereas to appear and refute the charge (Chariton, 5.8.1).

An examination of all the speeches in the novels—forensic, advisory, and celebrative—would only underscore the importance of this one form in the Greek novel, but the rhetorical forms do not stop with the speech. A sampling will suggest the wide variety of rhetorical forms taken up in the course of the several novels. There are fables, such as Longus' story of Syrinx (2.34); proverbs or maxims, which are especially frequent in Chariton (1.4.2; 12.6; etc.); and descriptions, such as Xenophon's description of Habrocomes' and Anthia's bridal chamber (1.8.2–3). Forms more familiar to students of the New Testament include letters (e.g., Achilles Tatius, 5.18.3–6; 20.5), miracle stories (e.g., Longus, 2.25.3–27.3), catalogues of hardships (e.g., Chariton, 6.2.10), oracles (e.g., Xenophon, 1.6.2), and even empty tomb stories (e.g., Chariton, 3.3.1–6).

But in addition to these various formal units in the novels there is an overall structural form to them as well. This structure entails humiliation of the novels' protagonists and then their exaltation at the end. A summary of the plot of these novels will point out this structure: hero and heroine come from aristocratic families but after they fall in love they lose this status and become slaves. In addition to the psychological humiliation of being treated as a slave they endure assorted physical hardships, usually as a result of their maintaining fidelity to their beloved. But in the end they are raised up to their former status by the aid of some gracious deity, after which they live happily ever after.

II. The Text: Chariton's *Callirhoe*

Chariton's *Callirhoe* is the least accessible in English translation, and it is closest in time to the major writings of the New Testament, the Gospels and the letters of Paul. For these reasons portions of this novel have been selected for presentation here.

Chariton's principal characters are Chaereas and Callirhoe. He introduces them as follows:

> Hermocrates, the general of Syracuse, the very one who conquered the Athenians, had a daughter, Callirhoe by name, an astonishingly beautiful young maiden and the delight of all Sicily. For her beauty was not human but divine, and not that of a sea or mountain nymph but of Aphrodite the Maiden herself (1.1.1–2).

> There was a certain Chaereas, a youth who surpassed all the others in his physique; just as sculptors and painters depict Achilles, Nireus, Hippolytus, and Alcibiades, so he looked. His father Ariston ranked second in Syracuse after Hermocrates (1.1.3).

These two fall in love in the following way:

> There was a public festival to Aphrodite, and virtually all the women went to her temple. And although Callirhoe had not ever appeared in public, her mother escorted her because her father had ordered her to worship the goddess.
> At that time, however, Chaereas was walking home from the gymnasium, shining like a star. For the flush of the wrestling school was adding to the luster of his appearance, as gold does to silver. By chance, therefore, at a narrow bend of the street they met and almost bumped into one another. The god Eros had arranged this incident in order that one might be seen by the other. And so at that instant they fell in love (1.1.4–6).

The two soon marry, but Chaereas' jealousy makes him susceptible to a plot by Callirhoe's former suitors who lead him to think that she is unfaithful. Angrily he kicks her. She falls unconscious, is thought dead, and is quickly and sumptuously buried. Tomb robbers, headed by the pirate Theron, break into the tomb, find her revived, and decide to carry her off along with funeral offerings. It is at this point that the many experiences begin which will in one way or another put their love to the test: separation, enslavement, brigands, judicial process, war.

Eventually, however, the two are reunited and return triumphantly to Syracuse. Their arrival causes quite a stir, and all Syracuse wants to hear their story. Chariton obliges with Chaereas giving a summary of their adventures. Chaereas' summary is detailed and in fact serves as a fine mini-version of the novel itself and is appropriate here. The translation picks up soon after Chaereas and Callirhoe arrive back in Syracuse.

> The crowd began to shout in unison, "Let's go to the assembly!" For they desired to see and hear them. The theatre was quickly filled with both men and women. But when only Chaeareas came, everybody, men and women, shouted again, "Summon Callirhoe!" Hermocrates acceded to the people in this and led his daughter in.
> Then the people first looked up to heaven and applauded the gods. In fact, they showed them more gratitude for this day than the day of their victory over the Athenians. Then they became divided, with the men praising Chaereas and the women Callirhoe, but then again they praised them both in unison, and this unity pleased the pair.

But because of her voyage and ordeal the crowd led Callirhoe out of the theatre immediately after she had greeted her native city, but the crowd detained Chaereas since they wished to hear the whole story of their journey. And so he began with the final episodes, not wishing to cause the people grief with the first and sad ones. But the people kept urging, "We ask you, begin from the beginning, tell us everything, leave nothing out."

Chaereas hesitated, being ashamed at many of the things that did not turn out as planned. Hermocrates, however, said: "Do not be ashamed, my child, even if you tell us something very grievous or bitter. For the splendid outcome overshadows all that went before. Besides, what is left unsaid carries with it the suspicion of something worse on account of the silence itself. And you are speaking to your native city and to your parents, whose affection for you both is evenly-balanced. In fact, the people themselves brought about your marriage, and we all know about your rival suitors' plot against your unfounded jealousy and how you unfortunately struck your wife, and that she, having appeared to have expired, was buried lavishly, whereas you on being brought to trial on a charge of murder voted against yourself since you wished to die with your wife. But the people acquitted you in the knowledge that what had happened was not intentional.

"And what happened after this has also been reported to us, namely that Theron the grave robber dug through the tomb at night and on finding Callirhoe alive put her along with the burial offerings in his pirate ship and sold her in Ionia, and that you went off in search of your wife. You did not find her but did come across the pirate ship on the sea and apprehended the other pirates who had died of thirst and so brought back only Theron, who was still alive, to the assembly. That scoundrel, after being tortured, was crucified. Then the city sent out a trireme and ambassadors on behalf of Callirhoe. Your friend Polycharmus willingly sailed out with you. These things we know. But you narrate to us what happened after you set sail from here."

Chaereas, taking up the narrative at this point, said: "After crossing the Ionic sea safely we landed on the property of a Milesian, Dionysius by name, who surpassed all the Ionians in wealth, family background, and reputation. He is the one who purchased Callirhoe from Theron for a talent. But do not fear! He did not enslave her. For he immediately made her who had been purchased mistress over his household. Moreover, while he loved her he did not dare to force himself on her since she was well-born. He could not, however, bear sending the one he loved back to Syracuse. But when Callirhoe perceived that she was pregnant by me, she wanted to save a citizen for you and so accepted the necessity of being married to Dionysius and cleverly disguised the parentage of the child in order that he might seem to have been born to Dionysius and that he might be reared honorably.

For, men of Syracuse, a wealthy citizen is being reared in Miletus by a man of high repute. Indeed, the family of that man is of high repute and Greek. Let us not bear him ill-will for this great inheritance.

"These things I learned later. At the time I landed on Dionysius' property and had high hopes since I had just seen a statute of Callirhoe in a temple. But at night Phrygian brigands ran down to the sea and set fire to our trireme. They murdered most of us, but they bound Polycharmus and me and sold us in Caria."

The crowd broke out in lamentation at this turn of events, and Chaereas said, "Permit me to be silent about what happened afterwards, for it is sadder than what went before."

But the crowd shouted, "Tell everything!"

And Chaereas said: "The man who purchased us, a slave of Mithridates, the governor of Caria, ordered us to dig, though we were chained. When some slaves killed the prison-guard, Mithridates ordered all of us crucified. But as I was being led away, Polycharmus, when he was about to be tortured, spoke my name, and Mithridates recognized it. (For he had been a guest of Dionysius in Miletus and was present when Chaereas was buried, since Callirhoe, on learning of the trireme and brigands, thought that I, too, had died and so had raised an expensive tomb for me.) Therefore, Mithridates quickly ordered me taken down from the cross just as I was coming to my end.

"Mithridates counted me among his dearest friends. He was eager to get Callirhoe back for me and made me write a letter to her. But because of the carelessness of the one who had been given the responsibility of delivering it Dionysius himself received the letter. He did not believe that I was alive but believed instead that Mithridates had designs on his wife. And so he immediately wrote a letter to the king accusing him of adultery.

"The king accepted the case and summoned all who were involved to himself. And so we went up to Babylon. Dionysius took Callirhoe and so made her admired and worshipped throughout Asia. Mithridates took me along. Once there we pleaded this remarkable case before the king. He quickly acquitted Mithridates, but promised a decision between Dionysius and me regarding Callirhoe, in the meantime entrusting her to the care of Queen Statira.

"How often do you imagine, men of Syracuse, that I resolved to die, since I was separated from my wife? But Polycharmus, my one true friend, saved me. Indeed, the king was not at all interested in the case because he was aflame with passion for Callirhoe. And yet, he neither seduced her nor used force on her.

Fortunately, Egypt revolted and started a savage conflict which, to my point of view, was the cause of remarkable blessings. The queen took Callirhoe along, but I heard a false report when

> someone said that she had been handed over to Dionysius. Consequently, wishing to punish the king, I deserted to the Egyptian leader and accomplished remarkable feats. For I myself conquered impregnable Tyre and after being appointed admiral defeated the Great King at sea and became master of Aradus where the king had put his wife as well as the wealth which you have seen. Therefore, I was able to appoint the Egyptian leader king over all Asia, were it not for the fact that he was killed while fighting on a separate front.
>
> "As far as the rest is concerned, I have made the Great King your friend by my giving him back his wife and by my sending back to the highest ranking of the Persians their mothers, brothers, wives, and daughters. I myself have brought here my noble Greek allies and those Egyptians who wished to come. And there will also sail from Ionia another expedition of yours, and the descendant of Hermocrates will lead it" (8.7.1–8.11).

Once finished with his rehearsal of what had happened, Chaereas makes several requests of the people which they consent to: Polycharmus is rewarded with Chaereas' sister as a wife and given part of the war spoils as a dowry, the Greek allies are awarded citizenship and given a talent each, and the Egyptians are given land on which to farm. The novel ends, however, with Callirhoe at the temple of Aphrodite:

> While the crowd was in the theatre Callirhoe, before going home, went to the temple of Aphrodite. She grasped the feet of the goddess, laid her face on them, loosed her hair, and after kissing them said: "Thank you, Aphrodite. For you have again shown me Chaereas in Syracuse where as a young maiden I saw him according to your will. I do not blame you, mistress, for what I have been through. That was my fate. I beg you: at no time separate me from Chaereas and also give us a life that is blessed and death that is shared" (8.8.15–16).

This selection is hardly a substitute for the reading the novel as a whole, much less all the novels. Still, this selection should give a sense of what the novels entail—their incidents, plot, values, and general atmosphere. It remains only to suggest how a knowledge of novels like Chariton's is of value for understanding early Christian literature.

III. The Greek Novel and Early Christian Literature

The number and variety of parallels between the Greek novels and early Christian literature are legion. The following sampling of these parallels only hints therefore at what a thorough investigation of this genre might accomplish for a more precise and subtle comprehension of early Christian literature in its historical context.

But first a word of justification: The evidence for earliest Christianity is too fragmentary and culturally alien to be fully understood without recourse to a clarifying and complementary set of roughly contemporary evidence. Typically, however, scholars have sought this evidence largely in Jewish sources; seldom has any scholar looked at the evidence of the novels. But whatever the Jewish roots of Christianity, the earliest Christians lived in a traditional culture and specifically that of the Hellenized *oikoumenē* of the early Roman Empire. The novels, products of this *oikoumenē*, often set their action precisely where Chrsitianity first took root and flourished: Barnabas' Antioch, Paul's Tarsus, John's Ephesus, Mark's Alexandria, Polycarp's Smyrna. But the point of comparison is not mere propinquity, for the novels provide an extensive, concrete, and coherent account of the traditional culture of the New Testament world. It is the novels' very comprehensiveness—their documenting the habits of thought and action that regulated life in the cities, agricultural areas, and outlying wilderness areas—that justifies their use for interpreting the parallel, but briefer, accounts in the New Testament and other early Christian literature.

And now to the parallels: The first set of parallels will focus on details in the novels and indicate how they corroborate, clarify, or even challenge our understanding of various early Christian texts. To keep the parallels roughly contemporary only the novels from the first and second centuries will be cited, and because of space the early Christian texts will be largely limited to the Gospels and letters of Paul.

Corroborating details in the novels are numerous. The counting of seeds at harvest time, familiar from the Parable of the Sower (Mark 4:3-8 pars.) in which some plants returned thirty, sixty, even a hundred fold, appears in Longus' novel, though in this case the number of seeds harvested barely equalled the number planted (Longus, 3.30.3). Again in Longus the shepherd Dryas leaves his flock in order to search for a lost sheep (Longus, 1.5.1-2), as does the shepherd in another parable (Matt 18:12-14 par.). The goatherd Daphnis knows his animals by name (Longus, 4.26.4), as does the shepherd in John 10:3.

On a more urban note the idle men of the marketplace whom the Jews use to apprehend Jason (Acts 17:5) are the same people Kynno persuades to arrest Habrocomes on a murder charge (Xenophon, 3.12.6). The cry "Great is Artemis of the Ephesians" which Paul hears (Acts 19:34) is on the lips of the Ephesian Anthia (Xenophon, 1.11.5). And Paul's remark about many athletes competing but only one taking the prize (1 Cor. 9:24) is repeated by Chariton (1.2.2-3). finally, Xenophon (1.11.2-6) corroborates the route of Paul's sea voyage along the coast of Asia Minor from Samos down to Cos and Rhodes (cf. Acts 20:15; 21:1).

Other details from the novels, however, do more than corroborate; they clarify various matters only briefly or vaguely mentioned in early Christian texts. For example, the teaching of Jesus which refers casually to a pit into which a sheep might fall (Matt 12:11) receives clarifying discussion in Longus. Villagers in the countryside around Mytilene on the island of Lesbos discover their flocks being attacked by a wolf. Consequently, they dig pits six feet across and four times as deep and then camoflage them by laying long branches over the top so as to capture the unsuspecting wolf (Longus, 1.11.1–2). Incidentally, instead of the wolf a goat tumbles in and is immediately pulled out (cf. 1.12.2–5). In other words, from Longus we learn the function of these pits, their dimensions and appearance, and the likelihood that a sheep or a goat might fall in.

Another example involves the Parable of the Talents (Matt 25:14–30 par.). In Matthew's version the first two slaves double their master's money (25:20–23), but in Luke's the profits are five and ten times the original investment (Luke 19:16–19). From Longus, however, the doubling of what is entrusted to slaves renders Matthew's version more typical or realistic. For Daphnis, having originally received fifty goats, was confident of getting his master's praise at an impending visit because he had doubled their number (Longus, 4.4.2–3; cf. 3.29.2). Note even the similar scene between master and slave. Lamon speaks for his son Daphnis as follows: "Master, this boy is the herder of your goats. You gave me fifty goats to tend as well as two males, and he has produced for you one hundred" (4.14.2–3).

The last of the details to be considered are those that challenge the usual interpretation of similar passages in early Christian literature. Thus in the Parable of the Prodigal Son (Luke 15:11–32) it is often noted how unusual it was—even unheard of—for the father to run out and greet his returning son (v. 20). Such action was beneath the dignity of an old man, it is claimed. But such behavior is precisely what we encounter in parallel situations in the novels. For example, when Chaereas and Callirhoe finally return to Syracuse, her father Hermocrates rushed on board ship and embraced his daughter (Chariton, 8.6.8). Likewise, when Daphnis' real identity is learned, his brother Astylos runs to greet him and hugs him (Longus, 4.23.1; cf. 2.30.1; 4.36.3; cf. also Achilles Tatius, 1.4.1; 7.16.3). In other words, instead of claiming the uniqueness of a detail in the parable, it may be more beneficial to see this detail as conforming to a social convention of how people greeted those they had long supposed had died. Indeed, few passages would benefit as much as this parable from a thorough comparison with the novels, for not only are there parallels to the initial moment of greeting but also descriptions of the following celebration (Luke 15:22–25; cf. Longus, 2.30–37; 4.26) as well as consideration of the delicate matter of what this returning son means to the other brother (Luke 15:25–32; cf. Longus, 4.24.3–4).

But fortuitous details—whether corroborating, clarifying, or challenging—hardly exhaust the utility of the novels for the interpreter of early Christian literature. Their real value lies in the complete and coherent account of Greco-Roman life that emerges on page after page of the novels. To be sure, the world of the novels is not always accurate and objective, given their penchant for an occasional miracle or the wildly improbable, not to mention various, usually aristocratic, biases. Still, the traditional world of the early Empire, both in its basic institutions and its countless and specific conventions of thought and action, shines through. It is thus this world in its totality and not just details that can help us interpret the New Testament.

Two examples: The first concerns epistolary conventions. Scholars have benefitted enormously from papyrus letters as well as from theoretical treatments of the letter in their investigations of the formulae and types found in Paul's letters. The novels, however, also contain many letters which scholars might use in their analyses.

These letters show many of the usual features of ancient letters: the simple word "greetings" in the salutation (Chariton, 8.4.5; Xenophon, 2.5.1; Achilles Tatius, 1.3.6), which we find outside Paul's letters in Acts 15:23 and Jas 1:1; the sending of greetings to specific individuals in the closing portion of the letter (Chariton, 8.4.6), which are so frequent in Paul's letters (e.g., Rom 16:3–16); and assurances that the letter is in the sender's hand (Chariton, 8.4.6), which also appear in 1 Cor 16:21 and Phlm 19.

But more important than these rather common epistolary formulae which the letters in the novels illustrate are the narrative contexts of these letters. Here are descriptions of the conventions regarding writing, sending, and reading letters which are otherwise quite rare. In other words, the letters are in context—and in a context which often parallels that of Paul's letters. For example, Chaereas writes his letter to Callirhoe with tears (Chariton, 4.6.6), as does Paul in one of his letters to the Corinthians (2 Cor 2:4). Furthermore, the sending of slaves with letters is frequent (Xenophon, 2.12.1; cf. Achilles Tatius, 1.3.5; 4.11.1), but in one instance the description permits a closer look. After Chaereas wrote his letter, Mithridates, his host, arranges for its delivery by having his most trusted slave and steward, Hyginus, carry the letter to Miletus (Chariton, 4.5.1). Similarly, the deutero-Pauline letter of Ephesians refers to the slave Tychicus, the bearer of the letter, as a trusted assistant (Eph 6:21–22). Callirhoe, however, sends her letter to Dionysius through her friend, Queen Statira, and gives her further oral messages to deliver (Chariton, 8.4.9; cf. Achilles Tatius, 5.21.1). Note that Tychicus also has oral messages concerning Paul in addition to the letter (Eph 6:21).

What is especially informative, however, are the detailed accounts of the recipients reading their letters. One passage deserves quotation in full: When Dionysius received Callirhoe's letter from the queen (cf. Chariton, 8.5.12), he "returned home and locked himself in his room and on recognizing Callirhoe's handwriting kissed the letter. Then he grasped it to his breast and held it a long time, unable to read it on account of his tears. But after weeping he began to read it with difficulty and first of all kissed the name 'Callirhoe.' But when he came to the words 'to Dionysius benefactor,' he said, 'Oh, no! I am no longer your "husband," for you are my benefactor. Indeed what worthwile thing have I done for you?' He was, however, delighted at the letter's apologetic tone and reread its contents over and over again, for they suggested that she had left him unwillingly" (8.5.13–14).

Three points merit discussion in light of passages in the New Testament. First, that Dionysius recognized Callirhoe's handwriting is a frequent initial reaction (see also Xenophon, 2.10.1; Achilles Tatius, 5.18.2), but in this case there is more behind it. Earlier Dionysius had suspected that a letter to Callirhoe from Chaereas was a forgery (cf. 4.6.1–2). Hence Callirhoe has good reason to say in her letter to Dionysius: "I am writing this message in my own hand" (8.4.6). This authenticating signature recalls Paul's similar practice, as known from 1 Cor 16:21; Gal 6:11; and Phlm 19; but especially relevant is the somewhat parallel case of 2 Thessalonians. Here, too, there is suspicion of forged letters (2 Thess 2:2) and hence the appropriateness of an emphatic authenticating signature (2 Thess 3:17).

Second, Dionysius' kissing the letter, grasping it to his breast, and holding it there—all as if Callirhoe herself were present in the letter—is a touching verification of the epistolary convention that the writer was present in the letter, at least in spirit if not in body (cf. also Achilles Tatius, 5.20.5). For early Christian examples of this convention, see 1 Cor 5:3; 1 Thess 2:17; and 2 John 12.

Third, Dionysius' pausing over the significance of the title "benefactor" in Callirhoe's salutation is also of interest, for scholars have long suspected that Paul's use of the title "apostle" in the salutations of some letters (1–2 Corinthians, Galatians) but not in others, such as Phil 1:1 which has "slave," is an indication of Paul's differing relationships with his churches. Dionysius' sensitivity to the title "benefactor" and what that means for his relationship with Callirhoe confirms these suspicions.

A second example comes from an especially rich vein in the novels: their extensive and nuanced treatment of slavery. In them appear the whole range of slaves, from such powerful stewards as Leonas (Chariton, 1.12.8) to such despised goatherds of the hills as Lampo (Xenophon, 2.9.2). The range of experiences is likewise full, including unspeakably cruel punishments (Xenophon, 2.6.3–5) and sexual abuse (Achilles Tatius, 5.17.4–10) as well as the ultimate reward of achieving freedom (Longus, 4.33.2).

The value of these data for interpreting the New Testament is immense, but I wish to concentrate on some very specific conventions regarding masters and slaves since they demonstrate the importance of this pervasive social experience for appreciating, say, the Christological reflections in the so-called Philippians hymn (Phil 2:6–11).

One convention becomes apparent in Chariton's novel. Callirhoe, after her sale to Leonas, Dionysius' steward, is on this aristocrat's rural property. She meets her master for the first time when he travels out to this property in order to inspect his herds and crops. They see one another in a temple of Aphrodite on this property. Her beauty astounds him, and he says: "'Be gracious, Aphrodite, and may your appearing to me be a good omen!' Leonas, however, spoke up just as Dionysius was falling to his knees, and he said: 'This woman, master, is the newly-purchased slave. Don't be confused. And, as for you, woman, come forward to your master.' Callirhoe, accordingly, at the name 'master' bowed low" (Chariton, 2.3.5–6).

The parallel between this passage and the hymn is obvious. Callirhoe's bending down at the mention of the word "master" is clearly the social convention that grounds the bending of knees of those in heaven, on earth, and under the earth at the mention of the name "Jesus," their master (Phil 2:10–11).

Moreover, another parallel with the hymn further clarifies the social conventions that lie behind it and so contribute to its meaning and truth. A little later in the story Callirhoe's free birth becomes known to Dionysius and he orders that she be treated with every consideration. His conduct is also motivated by his love for her and his intentions of marrying her. And with the aid of a slave woman he is able finally to get her consent.

At this point, however, her first husband, Chaereas, has reached Miletus in search of Callirhoe and chances upon the temple of Aphrodite where he sees a golden statue of Callirhoe which Dionysius had offered to the goddess. At the sight of the statue Chaereas "became dizzy and fell. The temple attendant, however, saw him and brought him water. After reviving him, she said: 'Cheer up, child. The goddess has startled many others, for she is a deity given to appearing and shows herself visibly. Indeed, this is a sign of great benefit to you. Do you recognize the golden statue? It is of a woman who was a slave, but Aphrodite has made her mistress of us all'" (3.6.3–4).

Callirhoe's experience of becoming a slave but later being made mistress of all in Dionysius' household illustrates the remarkable change of status a slave might undergo, but it also provides a more fundamental parallel with the hymn, as Jesus, too, after becoming a slave (Phil 2:7) was later made master of all (vv. 9–10).

Xenophon narrates a similar reversal of status. While a slave in the household of Apsyrtos, Habrocomes soon arouses the desire of the daughter Manto. When Apsyrtos is away, she sends a seductive letter to

Habrocomes, but he rejects her offer. When her father returns, she feigns rape out of spite for Habrocomes and has her father punish him cruelly and put him in a guarded room. Eventually, Manto is married off, and Apsyrtos finds the letter she had written. Then he "realized that he had punished Habrocomes unjustly. Consequently, he immediately ordered a slave to release and bring him to him. Habrocomes, having already suffered terrible and pitiable punishment, fell at Apsyrtos' knees. But Apsyrtos raised him up and said: 'Cheer up, young man. I condemned you unjustly, having been persuaded by my daughter's words. But now I will make you a free man instead of a slave, and I give to you my household to rule, and I will procure for you a daughter of one of the citizens to be your wife. As for you, do not bear a grudge for what has happened, for I did not knowingly treat you unjustly'" (Xenophon, 2.10.1–2).

To be sure, Habrocomes is not master but as Apsyrtos' steward he nonetheless rules "all in the household" (cf. 2.10.3–4). Here, then, is the precise social convention that the author of the Philippians hymn used to make credible his central Christological claim: just as a Callirhoe or a Habrocomes could have their status reversed so quickly and completely, so could the author of the hymn assert on the religious plane that Jesus, after becoming a slave and dying the horrible slavish death of crucifixion, could have been raised up by God and given the status of master over all in creation (Phil 2:7–11).

In other words, the conventions of bowing down at the name of the master and of slaves being made masters (or given positions of authority) provide the social reality that renders the religious claims about Jesus meaningful and true—meaningful in the sense of giving them a coherent context and true in the sense of their being true to experience. Accordingly, the value of the novels for interpreting early Christian literature is beyond doubt, if they deepen our understanding of its central confession, that Jesus Christ is Master (Phil 2:11).

IV. Annotated Bibliography

The single best volume on the novels as a whole is T. Hägg, *The Novel in Antiquity* (Oxford: Blackwell, 1983). It is comprehensive, balanced, and has an up-to-date bibliography. Other general works include: E. Rohde, *Der griechische Roman und seine Vorläufer* (Leipzig: Breitkopf and Härtel, ³1914); B. Perry, *The Ancient Romances: A Literary-Historical Account of Their Origins* (Berkeley: University of California, 1967); B. Reardon, *Courants littéraires grecs des IIe et IIIe siècles après J.-C.* (Paris: Les belles Lettres, 1971) 309–403; and two books by G. Anderson: *Eros Sophistes: Ancient Novelists at Play* (Chico, CA: Scholars, 1982) and *Ancient Fiction: The Novel in the Graeco-Roman World* (Totowa, NJ: Barnes & Noble, 1984). For short, general accounts, see B. Reardon, "The Greek Novel," *Phoenix* 23 (1969) 291–301, and E. Bowie, "The Greek

Novel" in *The Cambridge History of Classical Literature. Vol. 1. Greek Literature* (eds. P. Easterling and B. Knox; New York: Cambridge, 1985) 683–99. For further bibliography, see G. Sandy, "Recent Scholarship on the Prose Fiction of Classical Antiquity," *Classical World* 67 (1974) 321–59; for more recent work, see the bibliographies of Hägg, 235–50, and Bowie, "Novel," 877–86.

Of the many specialized studies of the novel the following were cited in this study: T. Hägg, *Narrative Technique in Ancient Greek Romances: Studies of Chariton, Xenophon Ephesius, and Achilles Tatius* (Stockholm, 1971); K. Kerényi, *Die griechisch-orientalische Romanliteratur in religions-geschichtlicher Beleuchtung* (Tübingen, 1927); R. Merkelbach, *Roman und Mysterium in der Antike* (Munich and Berlin, 1962); K. Barwick, "Die Gliederung der *narratio* in der rhetorischen Theorie und ihre Bedeutung für die Geschichte des antiken Romans," *Hermes* 63 (1928) 261–87. Studies cited on writings related to the novel include: F. Jouan, "Les thèmes romanesques dans L'*Euboïcos* de Dion Chrysostome," *Revue des études greques* 90 (1977) 38–46; F. Millar, "The World of the Golden Ass," *Journal of Roman Studies* 101 (1981) 63–75; S. West, "*Joseph and Aseneth:* A Neglected Greek Romance," *Classical Quarterly* 24 (1974) 70–81; S. Schierling and M. Schierling, "The Influence of the Ancient Romances on the *Acts of the Apostles*," *Classical Bulletin* 54 (1978) 81–88.

Individual studies on Chariton's *Callirhoe:* B. Perry, "Chariton and his Romance from a Literary-historical Point of View," *American Journal of Philology* 51 (1930) 93–134; A. Papanikolaou, *Chariton-Studien. Untersuchungen zur Sprache und Chronology der griechischen Romance* (Göttingen, 1973); M. Laplace, "Les Légendes troyennes dans le 'Roman' de Chariton, *Chaeréas et Callirhoé*," *Revue des études greques* 93 (1980); B. Reardon, "Theme, Structure, and Narrative in Chariton," *Yale Classical Studies* 27 (1982) 1–27; and P. van der Horst, "Chariton and the New Testament," *Novum Testamentum* 25 (1983) 348–55. See also the valuable introduction and commentary in the translation of K. Plepelits, *Chariton von Aphrodisias, Kallirhoe* (Stuttgart, 1976).

Individual studies on Xenophon's *Ephesian Tale:* K. Bürger, "Zu Xenophon von Ephesus," *Hermes* 27 (1892) 36–87; H. Gärtner, "Xenophon (Nr. 11)," in Pauly-Wissowa's *Realencyclopädie der classischen Altertumswissenschaft* 2. Reihe IX (1967) 2055–89; T. Hägg, "Die Ephesiaka des Xenophon von Ephesus—Original oder Epitome," *Classica et Mediaevalis* 27 (1966) 118–61; A. Scarcella, "Les structures socio-économiques du roman de Xénophon d'Éphèse," *Revue des études grecques* 90 (1977) 249–62; J. Griffiths, "Xenophon of Ephesus on Isis and Alexandria," in *Hommages à Maarten J. Vermaseren* (ed. M. de Boer and T. Edridge; 3 vols.; Leiden, 1978) 1.409–37; and G. Schmeling, *Xenophon of Ephesus* (Boston, 1980).

Individual studies on Achilles Tatius' *Clitophon and Leucippe:* D. Durham, "Parody in Achilles Tatius," *Classical Philology* 33 (1938) 1–19. See also the valuable introduction and commentary in the translation of K. Plepelits, *Achilles Tatios, Leucippe und Klitophon* (Stuttgart, 1980).

Individual studies on Longus' *Daphnis and Chole:* H. Chalk, "Eros and the Lesbian Pastorals of Longus," *Journal of Hellenic Studies* 80 (1960) 32–51; M. Mittelstadt, "Longus: Daphnis and Chloe and Roman Narrative Painting," *Latomus* 26 (1967) 752–61; A. Scarcella, "Realtà e letteratura nel paesaggio sociale ed economico del romanzo di Longo sofista," *Maia* 22 (1970) 103–31; B.

Effe, "Longos. Zur Functionsgeschichte der Bukolik in der römischen Kaiserzeit," *Hermes* 110 (1982) 65–84; R. Hunter, *A Study of Daphnis and Chloe* (Cambridge, 1983); and B. MacQueen, "Longus and the Myth of Chloe," *Illinois Classical Studies* 10 (1985) 119–34. See also the valuable introduction and commentary in the translation of O. Schönberger, *Longos, Hirtengeschichten von Daphnis und Chloe* (Berlin, 1960).

Individual studies on Heliódorus' *Ethiopian Tale*: J. Morgan, "History, Romance, and Realism in Heliodorus," *Classical Antiquity* 1 (1982) 221–65; G. Sandy, *Heliodorus* (Boston, 1982); and J. Winkler, "The Mendacity of Kalasiris and the Narrative Strategy of Heliodorus' *Aithiopika*," *Yale Classical Studies* 27 (1982), 93–158.

A note on translations: The University of California Press will soon publish translations of all the novels under the editorship of B. Reardon of the University of California, Irvine. In the meantime, there are the translations of M. Hadas: *Three Greek Romances: Longus, Xenophon, Dio Chrysostom* (Indianapolis, 1953) and *Heliodorus: An Ethiopian Romance* ((Ann Arbor, 1957). Achilles Tatius and Longus are available in the Loeb Classical Library, and Chariton has been translated by W. Blake, *Chariton's Chaereas and Callirhoe* (Ann Arbor, 1939).

Since writing this chapter two studies have been finished which not only have more extensive bibliographical references, but are also excellent examples of what can be done in relating the Greek novels to the writings of the New Testament, in particular the book of Acts: Richard I. Pervo, *Profit with Delight: The Literary Genre of the Acts of the Apostles* (Philadelphia: Fortress, 1987), and Douglas R. Edwards, *Acts of the Apostles and Chariton's Chaereas and Callirhoe* (Ph.D. Dissertation, Boston University, 1987).

www.ingramcontent.com/pod-product-compliance
Lightning Source LLC
Chambersburg PA
CBHW021811220426
43662CB00006B/274